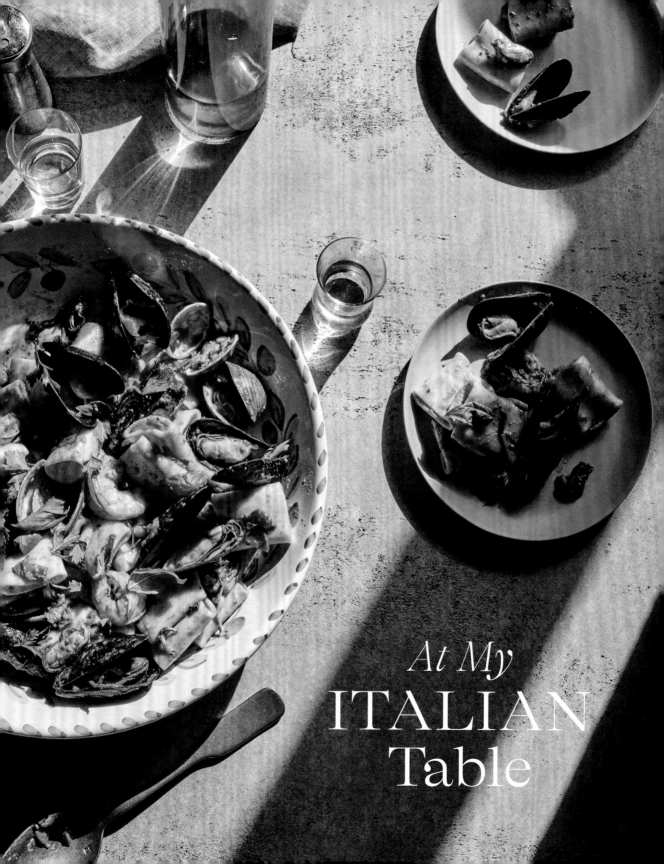

At My
ITALIAN
Table

At My ITALIAN Table

Family Recipes from My Cucina to Yours

Laura Vitale

With RACHEL HOLTZMAN

Photographs by Lauren Volo

CLARKSON POTTER/PUBLISHERS

NEW YORK

Published in the United States by Clarkson Potter/
Publishers, an imprint of the Crown Publishing
Group, a division of Penguin Random House LLC,
New York.
ClarksonPotter.com

CLARKSON POTTER is a trademark and POTTER
with colophon is a registered trademark of Penguin
Random House LLC.

Library of Congress Cataloging-in-Publication Data
Names: Vitale, Laura, 1986– author. | Holtzman,
    Rachel, author. Title: At my Italian table: family
    recipes from my cucina to yours / Laura Vitale,
    creator and author of Laura in the Kitchen
    with Rachel Holtzman. Description: New York:
    Clarkson Potter, [2024] | Includes index. |
    Identifiers: LCCN 2023010673 (print) | LCCN
    2023010674 (ebook) | ISBN 9780593579862
    (hardcover) | ISBN 9780593579879 (ebook)
    Subjects: LCSH: Cooking, Italian. | LCGFT:
    Cookbooks. Classification: LCC TX723 .V5648
    2024 (print) | LCC TX723 (ebook) | DDC
    641.5945—dc23/eng/20230317
LC record available at https://lccn.loc.
    gov/2023010673
LC ebook record available at https://lccn.loc.
    gov/2023010674

ISBN 978-0-593-57986-2
Ebook ISBN 978-0-593-57987-9

Printed in China

Editor: Raquel Pelzel | Editorial assistant: Bianca Cruz
Designer: Laura Palese
Production editor: Patricia Shaw
Production manager: Heather Williamson
Compositors: Merri Ann Morrell and Hannah Hunt
Food stylist: Mira Evnine | Food stylist assistants:
Megan Litt and Lauren Utvich
Prop stylist: Maeve Sheridan | Prop stylist
assistants: Tsering Dolma and Ashleigh Sarbone
Photo assistants: Christina Zhang and Sam Schmieg
Copy editor: Kate Slate | Proofreader: Liana
Faughnan | Indexer: Elizabeth T. Parson
Publicist: Erica Gelbard | Marketer: Stephanie Davis

10 9 8 7 6 5 4 3 2 1

First Edition

TO NONNA,
*forever and
always my biggest
inspiration, in and
out of the kitchen*

CONTENTS

Introduction 9

The Italian Pantry, Kitchen
Staples & Tools 15

Before Dinner Snacking

(Because We Don't Believe in Formal Canapés Around Here)

22

Quick & Easy Mains

(For When Time & Patience Are Short but Dinner Is a Priority)

70

An Italian Sunday

(Or Any Day Where You Want to Shimmy into Nonna Mode)

127

Seriously Good Vegetable Sides & Salads

(That I Often Eat as Dinner with Some Crusty Bread)

191

Sweet Endings

(Because No Self-Respecting Italian Would Dare Have a Special Meal Without One)

226

INTRODUCTION

Growing up in Naples, Italy, I was taught from a very young age that to eat was not just to fill your belly. Food was meant to be something delicious and satisfying, to be sure, but it was also how Italians connected with one another, marked moments in time, or simply just *lived*. There was the deep comfort of waking up in the morning and sipping a bowl of sweet zuppa di latte with my nonno, who had just gotten back from the docks, or sitting down to a steaming plateful of my nonna's spaghetti aglio e olio after school—my paternal grandparents having helped raise me as though I was their own to help my young parents.

There was the buzz of excitement from everyone gathering at my namesake, Nonna Laura's, for Sunday pranzo, all the cousins racing for the next fresh batch of cauliflower fritters coming out of the pan, then grazing for hours over bracioletti al sugo and zucchini parmigiana. On birthdays, it was the cherished honor of Nonna cooking your favorite meal *and* dessert (pasta al forno, a side of broccoli rabe, and pastiera napoletana, forever and always). And when someone passed, it was walking with Nonna to drop off that family's favorite cake of hers (usually her famous olive oil apple snack cake or fruit crostata), so they could savor something that brought them joy. "There is no answer that food doesn't provide," she would say.

"There is no answer that food doesn't provide," she would say.

The slab of tomato pie I'd grab from the bakery on my way to school, the paper bags of piping hot zeppole e panzerotti we'd munch as we walked home from the beach, the caprese that was on everyone's table the minute the weather turned warm—these were the memories of my childhood. And when I think about them, I can certainly taste each and every one of those dishes—which is why their recipes are now in this book—but more than anything, I remember the way that each of these special moments touched my soul. And that's exactly what saved me.

When I was twelve, I came to the States to visit my dad, who had been living in Philadelphia with his new wife. I was there to celebrate the birth of my twin half-siblings and was supposed to stay only through Christmas, but due to unforeseen circumstances, my parents felt it was best for me to remain indefinitely. What began as an extended vacation turned into a completely new way of life—a new family, a new house, not to mention a new language in a new country. While I knew that my dad would care for me, it felt like only a small solace compared with losing the warmth and security of my mother, Nonna, and Nonno. For a young child— for anyone, really—it was abrupt and difficult. I felt homesick for months, struggling to adjust and feeling lost and alone.

Then one afternoon, I was talking to my nonna—or sobbing, more like it—and I asked what she was cooking that day. "My Sunday sauce," she said, which made me even more

upset because in that moment, I could feel in the pit of my stomach how much I missed walking into her house on a Sunday morning and smelling the pot going on the stove. I told her that I was afraid I'd forget what it tastes like. To which she, very reasonably, said, "Why don't you just make it?" *Me? Make Nonna's Sunday sauce*?! It seemed like such an outlandish suggestion to try to cook this sacred recipe, until she added, "I'll teach you how." I grabbed the nearest piece of paper—a PECO energy bill—wrote down everything she instructed, and I handed my dad a list of ingredients to buy at Pathmark. Then I followed each step, exactly as she described them—no easy task, seeing as the woman cooks from intuition more than precise measurements. But far from feeling overwhelmed, I was overcome with the familiarity of it all: spending the day in the kitchen helping my grandmother or mother or godmother or aunts or uncles prepare whatever it was that was to be for lunch or dinner (or just a snack to eat while cooking—a staple of the Italian diet, and one that gets its own chapter here); the comforting universal sameness of peeling garlic and chopping onions; and then there was the deep, savory aroma of the sauce as the aromatics, braising meats, and simmering tomatoes began to come together. For the first time in a long time, I was home.

When I realized that the only thing that helped me to not feel sad was cooking, I started cooking a whole lot more. I'd call my nonna in the morning to see what she was making that afternoon, and little by little, I re-created all the dishes I grew up with, where just one smell brought me back to happiness and security. From fagioli a zuppa (beans bathed in a tomato and basil broth) to eggplants marinated in oil and vinegar with tons of garlic, I cooked my little heart out every single day. By the time I was fifteen, I had started working in my dad's pizzeria, where I could make a little money doing something that made me feel whole. As a

teen, I loved whipping up treats for my friends. And by my early twenties, when I was newly engaged and living with my now-husband, Joe, I was known as the girl who made giant batches of meatballs every Sunday and everyone would drop by unannounced knowing they would have plenty to snack on while watching football. Joe's family and our friends quickly learned that the place to have celebratory or holiday meals—or any meal, let's be honest—was at our house. And ever since the birth of our daughter, Mia, I've made sure that she knows that no matter how special or disappointing her day has been, there will be something delicious to preserve that moment into memory or to help it pass less painfully.

People always ask me when I knew that I wanted to cook for a living. And the truth is, never. I always thought I'd be a hairstylist or a makeup artist. But the reality is that cooking showed up for me when I needed something to hang on to. And ever since that moment in my life, I've made it my mission to share the power that food has to ease the difficult times and forever cement the good ones as memories. Whether it's lugging my electric skillet (page 20) to the garage because it's raining but my little sister just got dumped and needs her favorite eggplant and chicken cutlets, or making a pot of pastina in brodo for Mia because it's her favorite after-sledding meal, or sending my recipes out into the world so people can share them with their own families and create their own special moments, these are the reasons why I do what I do—because I know how these dishes, and the intentions behind them, make people feel. And because ultimately, life is made up of a collection of little things that bring us joy every day, and I'm going to celebrate the heck out of each and every one.

AT MY ITALIAN TABLE is exactly what is sounds like—it's all the recipes you need to capture the essence of what I think makes Italian meals so special. They're the simple staples made from the season's most anticipated ingredients that you can cook and enjoy over and over again because they never get old, that can be mixed and matched, that never apologize for needing only a good, crusty loaf of bread to make a complete dinner, and that rarely require more than one pot or pan, a few pantry items, and a little bit of hands-on time. They are the recipes that you reach for both when you want a satisfying and comforting but quick-to-come-together meal at the end of a long day, as well as those days when you have a little more to celebrate, or a little more time to savor in the kitchen.

I should know; these are the dishes from my everyday, very real (very Italian) life. (I jokingly call my house Villa Vitale because how we eat and live is like a slice of Italy in South Jersey.) That's something that means a lot to me and has come to mean a lot to my extended social media family. Every morning when I wish my online community a "Buongiorno" or "Good Morning"—which has become such a ritual that if I don't do it, I get thousands of messages wondering if I'm okay—it's in the spirit of sharing things from my life as genuinely and realistically as possible. These recipes are no exception. People sometimes think we Italians can't call it a meal unless it has fourteen courses. Sure, come over on Christmas Eve or Easter and I'd say you're probably right. But on a Monday? Not even close! I grew up watching my nonna— an Italian if ever there was one—setting out effortless meal after effortless meal using no more than five or six ingredients to create a beautiful dinner or lunch. There'd be bread on the table, some wine for Nonno, and maybe some fruit for dessert. But ultimately, simplicity was queen. Dinners, especially on a weeknight, don't need to be three-course

These are the dishes from my everyday, very real (very Italian) life.

meals. No one's got time for that! And no one's expecting that. Show me a kid who misses having sides with their pasta! No, when you've got a nourishing, delicious dish at the center of a meal, it IS the meal. One and done. That's exactly how I'm cooking for my own family week after week, and it's the same recipes you can now reach for depending on your mood, your preferences, and your time.

Now, weekends and special occasions?... that's a (slightly) different story, and those recipes live here, too. These dishes aren't necessarily more difficult than what I'm making during the week, but they might take a little longer to proof or braise in the oven or simmer away on the stove—which is really just hands-off time, if you think about it. And yes, maybe for these meals you're also throwing in a simple side or two, which believe me, I've got you covered for. And possibly a dessert. (Who are we kidding? DEFINITELY a dessert!) But the biggest difference between these dishes and the ones you'll be reaching for during the week is how you're making and serving them. They should hopefully be a reminder to breathe a little more deeply, move a little more slowly, and eat like you've got nowhere to be but here. It doesn't matter if you're cooking for four, for ten, or for yourself (heck yeah!), these recipes and their preparation *are* the moment.

To be honest, the same is true for any recipe in this book. And that's because many of them capture some of my favorite moments. From the time Uncle Tony took us to Sicily and introduced me to sweet, sour caponata; to the magical trip to Tuscany that changed my life (and my steak game) forever; to sitting on my nonno's lap, eating polenta and roasting chestnuts; to having hot chocolate so thick you eat it with a spoon for Santo Antonio; to simply spending all day in the kitchen rolling gnocchi, stuffing the dough for pizza ripiena, or lovingly stirring a pot of seafood risotto—these are the beautiful memories I want to hold on to for dear life, and the way I can do that is through these recipes.

But while this book is a celebration of my family, particularly Nonna and her legacy, it's also very much about the future. It's my most sacred duty to keep these traditions alive—for my dad, Papa Sal, who loves coming to my house, especially around the holidays, because it reminds him of his own childhood home; for Mia, so she will always be deeply connected to her past and so she's never farther from feeling comforted and loved than a handful of ingredients; and for you, so *you* can create your own memories. If just a fraction of my excitement and giddiness and affection and care comes through when you make these recipes for your family, then I will have done my job right. If you decide that you want to reach for these dishes because you believe that a Tuesday deserves as much special attention as a Sunday or because you made it to Thursday (what I like to call "Weekend Eve") after a week that felt a month long and think you deserve a treat, then you're really paying attention. And if you make an afternoon olive oil snack cake so everyone can have a little something before dinner, and maybe a pitcher of peaches in wine, then you've officially reached Nonna status. Now let's go make something tasty to eat!

Baci!
Laura

※

THE ITALIAN PANTRY, KITCHEN STAPLES & TOOLS

We Italians know how to do a lot with a little, and our pantries are no exception. Visit any nonna's kitchen and you won't find one of those glorified walk-in closets with matching baskets and those cute little labels. No, she'll have a tiny cupboard with just the essentials, plus a handful of go-tos in the fridge—and that's it. Anything else is coming fresh from the garden or the market. But with that tiny stash of staples—many of which you most likely already have—comes a huge range of dishes (this entire book is case in point). That's why I like to think of my pantry as the ultimate capsule wardrobe—you need only a few good pieces that you love, invest in the best you can, then endlessly mix and match. I'll never apologize for making the same great dishes over and over again, and the same goes for my ingredients. If I ask you to buy good anchovies, rest assured you're going to use 'em all! With just these pantry items on hand and a small market shop, I guarantee that you'll be able to get something delicious on the table, and quickly. I've listed some of my favorite brands here, too, where I think they make a difference.

Italian Pantry

Olive oil: I use Bertolli Light Taste olive oil for most of my cooking because it has a very mild flavor that won't get in the way of the other ingredients. For shallow-frying, I'll typically use Bertolli Extra Light Taste because it has essentially no flavor (although I don't use it for deep-frying because it's not as budget friendly as vegetable or canola oil; see next entry). And for drizzling and finishing dishes, I use California Olive Ranch Extra-Virgin Olive Oil (Medium), which has that classic, herbaceous olive oil flavor. Each recipe will specify which I've used.

Deep-frying oil: I use vegetable or canola oil because it has a high smoke point and is less expensive than olive oil.

Freshly ground black pepper: I use Tellicherry peppercorns in a grinder.

Salt: I use Morton coarse kosher salt unless otherwise stated. I'll occasionally use Maldon flaky sea salt and have specified in each recipe which is called for.

Red wine vinegar: I use the DeLallo brand. I suggest spending a couple extra dollars rather than buying the generic store brand, since those tend to have no flavor whatsoever.

Capers: I prefer capers packed in salt because they don't have the vinegary flavor of capers in brine and have a slightly firmer texture that I like, but if all you can find are capers in brine, it will be fine. Both kinds require rinsing before using.

Tuna: I use good-quality Italian tuna packed in olive oil and prefer the Tonnino brand. If you can't find Tonnino, go for any other tuna packed in olive oil (never water!).

Anchovies: I live and breathe for the Ortiz brand; I find them to be the best in every way—they're more flavorful (never fishy!), have a nice supple texture, practically melt when cooked down, and are the most affordable of the "nicer" brands. Also, since I will stop at nothing to make everyone anchovy lovers, I highly recommend dissolving your anchovies into butter whenever making something savory. They act like salt and make everything taste more like it should.

Olives: I find that Mezzetta makes a pretty good Kalamata olive, which happens to be my go-to black olive. (I buy them pitted.) They also have a nice Castelvetrano, which, to me, are the only acceptable green olives, which I buy not pitted because I think they have more flavor that way.

Parmigiano-Reggiano cheese: I buy a large wedge or block, then process it by adding it (in batches) to a high-powered blender and pulsing until it's finely grated. (Strangely, this doesn't work as well in a food processor.) I store it in an airtight container in the refrigerator, and when a measurement calls for grated Parm (unless otherwise stated), I'm measuring it from my grated stash. *Please take note: The measures in this book are based on this method.* If you're using a Microplane to grate your Parm, you'd need about three times the amount. The blender method, on the other hand, will save you time and money while also giving a better texture to your grated Parm.

Pecorino cheese: Pecorino is a sheep's milk cheese, versus Parm, which is made from cow's milk. It has a more pungent flavor than Parm, which is why I typically use it only in dishes where you want the pecorino to stand out (like Cacio e Pepe Arancini, page 30, and Pasta alla Nerano-ish, page 92). I also use the blender method for grating my pecorino.

Fresh whole-milk ricotta: This isn't necessarily something you need to have all the time, but if you do buy it, make sure it's labeled as "fresh" because it is thicker, denser, and "milkier" than regular ricotta. Most grocery stores will have a specialty cheese case by the deli counter (the same spot where you can find wedges or blocks of good Parm and other specialty cheeses), which is where you'll see fresh ricotta sold in what looks like a little basket. But if you can't find fresh ricotta in your market or an Italian deli, then just drain regular ricotta in a sieve lined with cheesecloth or a coffee filter overnight in the fridge and it will be great.

Canned plum tomatoes: I prefer San Marzano plum tomatoes. (Just be sure to peep for that DOP mark!) If a recipe calls for crushed tomatoes, I hand-crush plum tomatoes; I simply don't think any precrushed tomato is nearly as good as doing it yourself, namely because I believe you get a better texture and you can feel for the tough little pieces (where the stem attached to the tomato) and discard them.

Passata: This is essentially strained pureed tomatoes. I like Cento Traditional Passata.

Garlic: In most grocery stores there are two kinds of garlic: There's the kind over by the onions in the little mesh sleeves, usually with smaller heads. Don't buy those; they're always stale and the cloves are tiny. But over by the tomatoes and basil are the nice medium heads. They're going to have nice medium-size cloves, which are what are called for in these recipes. But honestly, so long as you're not using preminced garlic (because that's not garlic, no matter what you say), or prepeeled (it's already lost all its flavor), you're going to be okay.

Onions: I love a standard yellow onion. I'm low maintenance with this one.

Golden raisins: Sun-Maid is always my go-to brand, but any will do. Just make sure they aren't coated with any sugar or spices.

Pine nuts: They cost a small fortune but a little goes a long way! I store them in the freezer because it keeps them fresh for up to six months.

SEASONING FROM THE HEART

Something you'll notice in these recipes is that occasionally I won't give you an exact measure for salt and/or pepper. This is *not* because I couldn't be bothered. Rather, it's because I'm a firm believer in seasoning according to your preferences and the needs of the dish and your ingredients. Seasoning by heart, by intuition, whatever you want to call it, is the best way to learn how to season your food. In the places where it really matters, such as in baking recipes, I've got you covered. But otherwise, start small—because you can't come back from oversalting—and go from there. You'll know you've got it right when all the flavors pop and the dish really sings. The same goes for olive oil or anything else that gets drizzled or sprinkled. Go with what feels good to you and remember that a little extra never hurt anybody!

Canned cannellini beans: Truth is, I do prefer to cook my own cannellini beans from dried, and when I do that, I love to use the Camellia brand. But if buying canned, I love the DeLallo brand—though any (non-Italian) brand will do! And when cooking with canned beans, always drain and rinse them first.

Red pepper flakes: I do love and prefer Calabrian chile flakes, but I'm not picky about this one. Just don't use one you bought twelve years ago; they lose their flavor after about a year.

Dried Italian oregano: This I will be a little more finicky about because I feel like standard oregano has no flavor. So I will politely ask you to please get your hands on some Tutto Calabria dried oregano. I try to buy mine from Italy every year and bring it back, but Tutto Calabria makes a good one that I always have for backup!

Arborio rice: This is a short-grain rice that yields a rich, creamy end product that's perfect for risotto or boiling in chicken stock and finishing with way too much Parm when anyone needs a little comfort, and quickly. Any brand will do here!

Pasta: I always suggest that people have a few different styles of pasta in their pantry—a small shape such as ditalini, a medium tube pasta, such as penne rigate or rigatoni, and always a spaghetti and linguine. I am slightly picky about the brands because I do feel there is a difference. A few I love and use pretty much daily are Barilla, Anna, De Cecco, La Molisana, and Colavita. Occasionally I will splurge on even pricier brands because you really can tell the difference in both flavor and texture, but you can always find these affordable brands in the grocery store. Don't forget to stock up when they're on sale!

PERFECT PASTA

In my experience, the package directions for cooking pasta always deliver overcooked noodles. That's why in these recipes I typically advise you to remove 2 minutes from the package cook time, or 3 if you're finishing the pasta by simmering it in a sauce.

Good Italian bread (and mixed greens): My mother has lived by the phrase "No meal is complete without good bread and mixed greens." So, I always have mixed greens in the fridge and good artisan bread such as a crisp baguette, chewy ciabatta, or crusty Italian loaf in the freezer. Some people have a freezer full of ice cream; me, I have a freezer full of bread. Once you warm it back up in the oven—wrapped in foil, baked at 350°F for 10 minutes, then completely unwrapped for another 5 to 10 minutes—it will taste just like it did when it was freshly baked.

Bread crumbs: Progresso Plain bread crumbs are my staple! Anything store-bought is completely fine, so long as they're plain and not flavored.

All-purpose flour: King Arthur unbleached is my go-to.

Granulated sugar: Domino is hard to beat.

Vanilla bean paste: I like using paste versus extract because the flavor is superior to extract. But good-quality *pure* vanilla extract is fine (especially if you make your own, which I do every couple of years; see opposite).

Instant yeast: I use Saf brand; it never fails me! I like to buy a large bag's worth and keep it in a sealed container in the refrigerator, where it will stay fresh for 3 to 4 months.

Kitchen Staples & Tools

One thing you need to know about me is that I'm just not a fan of too many gadgets taking up precious real estate in my kitchen. I also have zero time for one-trick ponies, which is why you won't find any air fryer or Instant Pot options here. I always say you should stock your kitchen with things that you use over and over again. And just like I'd never have you buy an ingredient that you'll use only a little of and throw the rest away (blasphemy!), I assure you that these basics will get you through just about every recipe in this book. Now, a few things here are luxuries versus necessities—Nonna has never owned a stand mixer in her life—so use your judgment as to what you think you'll actually use and invest where you know it will count. You most likely already have a number of these items, and the rest will get you that much closer to cooking like a pro without all the fluff (and extra stuff).

7-quart Dutch oven: You'll use this for most of your cooking, especially when it comes to making tomato sauce, soups, and frying. It doesn't have to be expensive—Lodge and Crock-Pot both make really nice, affordable ones.

5-quart braiser: I use this to make all my sides, pasta, sauces—you name it! Again, no need to spend hundreds and hundreds of dollars on one.

12-inch skillet: Stainless steel or nonstick, the choice is yours. I prefer stainless steel, but some might argue that nonstick is a bit more user-friendly. All-Clad makes my favorite skillets; they last a lifetime.

Roasting pan: It doesn't necessarily need to be expensive, but I do like one with handles. Make sure it's big enough to fit two small chickens or one turkey, usually about 12 × 16 inches.

Half-sheet pans: Get yourself some good heavy-duty sheet pans and you'll be amazed at how often you'll use them—for roasting, storing, prepping, as platters, and especially when cooking outside on a grill. A typical half-sheet pan measures 18 × 13 inches.

The Only VANILLA EXTRACT you'll ever need

MAKES 1 CUP

5 vanilla beans
(I like Madagascar beans)
8 ounces 80-proof vodka

Use the tip of a paring knife to split the vanilla beans down the center lengthwise. Add them to an 8-ounce jar or bottle with a fitted lid (I like the bottles with a swing top stopper) and pour the vodka over the top. Cover and store it in a cool, dark spot (like the bottom of the pantry) for 6 months, minimum. Give it a shake every couple days. It will last forever.

Tostapane: I love a tostapane (a stovetop bread grill) for giving my bruschetta and charred bread a true char flavor that's hard to beat. They're easiest found online.

Electric skillet: A frying game changer! Unlike a deep fryer, it's light and portable, you can use it for other types of cooking, and it's very easy to keep clean. And I use it to fry outside—or in my garage, if it's raining—so that I don't have to scrub down my stove, my backsplash, my hood, my floor, and anything else within five feet of the hot oil. It doesn't have to be expensive; just look for one that has a temperature gauge and is about 12 × 15 inches so there's plenty of room.

Food processor: This is one of the few kitchen gadgets I allow to have a permanent spot on my kitchen counter. It doesn't have to be the most expensive one on the market, just good enough to get the job done and compact enough to fit in your kitchen.

Blender: BlendTec is the best because of how powerful and durable the motor is. I've had mine for ten years!

Food mill: No need to splurge on anything pricey. I bought mine in Italy ten years ago for 2 euros.

Hand mixer: Any brand will do, but I do prefer my cordless KitchenAid mixer so I don't have to mess with finding an outlet.

Stand mixer: You can use a hand mixer for pretty much anything you'd use a stand mixer for, but if you want to invest, I suggest a KitchenAid—I've had mine for seventeen years and it's still going strong!

FRY ME TO THE MOON

One very important lesson to learn for making these recipes: Frying outside is the best way to fry! Especially in the summer, I like taking my electric skillet outside so I can enjoy the fresh air and chat with my guests while whatever I'm making is sizzling away. My husband keeps the wineglasses full, and everyone can help themselves to crisp, golden goodies as I load them onto a plate. I love cooking in front of people because it starts the night with a *bang*. To me, it's the ideal way to spend time with friends.

Pasta roller attachment or pasta machine: There are a few models and manufacturers out there. I have the Antree Pasta Maker, which attaches to any standard KitchenAid mixer, and I've been using it for years and years.

Fish grilling basket: This keeps seafood from falling through the grill grates; it also allows you to turn everything at once (without burning the hair off your arms).

Good-quality knives: Your knives should be something to invest in; they will last you a lifetime (as long as you never put them through the dishwasher!). You don't need to buy a set with forty-nine different knives, though; you need just a chef's knife, a serrated knife, and a paring knife. I use an electric sharpener for all my knives (good, sharp knives are key for more efficient AND safer prep).

Cutting boards: My rule is: a big, thick wooden board for veggies; a nonslip plastic one for meats and proteins; and a plastic one for just fruits. I never cut raw meat on a wooden board because it's too difficult to sanitize afterward, and I never cut fruit on a veggie board (I don't want my watermelon to taste like onions!), but you do you.

Bench scraper: A bench scraper is like my assistant in the kitchen—I scoop up all my chopped ingredients with it; I use it to clean my work surface and cutting boards; it helps with kneading and just about everything in between! I recommend having a straight-edged metal scraper and a plastic one with a curved side for scraping out batters and doughs from a bowl.

Microplane: Microplane brand is king!

Glass mixing bowls: Get a set of these. Having a number of different sizes means you'll always have a bowl for prepping, cooking, and serving.

Wooden spoons: Or as we like to call them, Nonna's favorite weapons. You'll use these for everything from stirring sauces to making cake batter. They're another thing you'll have forever and a day if you take care of them properly, such as never running them through the dishwasher.

Pepper mill: Using whole peppercorns makes such a difference in a dish, which is why you want a good pepper mill to grind it up to taste. I like that it can be adjusted for some coarse or finely ground pepper action.

In-oven thermometer: It's important to make sure that your oven is properly calibrated. If you notice that your oven is running a little under or over temp (for the most part; some ovens cycle on and off to maintain a set temperature), you will most likely need to adjust your cook times accordingly.

OTHER ESSENTIALS

Instant-read thermometer

Clip-on thermometer

Muffin tin

Mandoline

Silicone spatula

Tongs

Spider

Potato ricer

Kitchen spider

Rolling pin: A classic one with handles is my favorite!

Whisk: A balloon whisk is what I use most often, but a flat whisk can come in handy when you need to whisk things quickly.

9 x 13-inch baking pan

9-inch tart pan with removable bottom

8- and 9-inch springform pans

9-inch square metal cake pan

10-inch round baking pan

Loaf pan

Before Dinner SNACKING

(Because We
DON'T Believe in
Formal CANAPÉS
Around Here)

PEOPLE ARE *always asking me what I miss*

the most about Italy. Besides the obvious (my family, the food), I like to say that I miss the *mindset*. You've got to love a place where even before you sit down for a meal—heck, even before you start cooking!—there's a meal. There's always gonna be a little something to munch on, like a deliciously fluffy cloud of focaccia barese at the corner bar, a paper bag full of fritto misto that you grab from the street vendor on the way home, or a slab of bruschetta with tomatoes from the garden and way too much olive oil drizzled over top. It's nothing fancy, nothing that took a terribly long time to prepare, nothing that even requires a knife and fork, but always something that hits the spot in the most intensely satisfying way. I think that we Italians do this for a couple reasons: It gets you excited about the meal to come, but it also sets the mood.

I consider the offer of a predinner snack an invitation to unwind, to breathe a little more deeply, and to connect. When my girlfriends come over, we're making antipasti and soaking peaches in wine before we're even *thinking* about cooking. Off the bat, we're chatting and relaxing and having a good time, and no one gets the wrong idea that we're about to sit down to a stuffy four-course meal with napkins in our laps and everyone on their best behavior. During the week, a predinner snack might just be a simple bowl of whipped ricotta with Bugles for dipping and a spritz for sipping on my back porch with my husband, which, let me tell you, is about as close to heaven as it gets. No matter how many or few people are coming over, or how special the occasion, thoughtful snacks are a must in this household, and these recipes will deliver every time. Serve them on their own or in any combination, with dinner or on the side, with chilled wine or a spritz—whatever speaks to you, your appetite, and the moment. You can't go wrong. So as my nonna would say, "Go ahead, have a little something." ✳

Nonna's Famous
Marinated Eggplant

Extra-light olive oil for
the grill (optional)

4 small to medium firm
Italian eggplants (about
2 pounds; see Note), cut
lengthwise into slices
¼ inch thick (I use a
mandoline for this)

⅔ cup red wine vinegar

2 cups extra-light olive oil

Kosher salt

4 garlic cloves, finely
minced

Handful of fresh Italian
parsley (about ½ cup
loosely packed), finely
minced

Red pepper flakes

NOTE

*I suggest using Italian eggplants
for this dish because they are smaller and
firmer, which means fewer seeds,
which means less bitterness. They also don't
fall apart as much when cooked.
If you can't find Italian eggplant, just buy
the smallest and firmest eggplant
you can find.*

It's just a fact that these garlicky, pickle-y, oily slices of tender eggplant have the ability to transform even the biggest eggplant skeptic. There was never (ever) a day when Nonna didn't have a fresh batch in the fridge, and we'd pile slices on giant pieces of crusty bread for lunch. Now I keep a container in my own fridge all summer long, which comes in handy for snacking on throughout the day. You could also use this recipe to make marinated raw zucchini, grilled pumpkin, or even fresh sardines, but it's agreed by all that eggplant is the fan favorite.

✳ Preheat a grill (or grill pan) to medium-high heat.

✳ Brush the grates (or pan) with oil if you're concerned about the eggplant sticking. Add the eggplant slices (no need to brush them with any oil) and grill until they develop deep brown grill marks, 2 to 3 minutes per side. Transfer the eggplant to a plate and set aside to cool.

✳ In a shallow bowl, combine the vinegar and ⅔ cup water. Add the cooled eggplant and stir to coat in the vinegar mixture. Set aside for 15 minutes.

✳ In a medium baking dish (mine is an 8 × 9-inch oval), add a couple tablespoons of the oil. Lay the eggplant slices in a single layer, season with a pinch of salt, then sprinkle with a bit of garlic, some parsley, and a pinch of pepper flakes. Add a bit more oil and continue this process, making sure that the final layer of eggplant is nearly submerged in the oil.

✳ Cover the dish with plastic wrap and pop in the fridge for a minimum of 6 hours, but ideally overnight.

✳ Allow the eggplant to come to room temperature for 15 minutes before serving. (The olive oil may have solidified when chilled; don't worry, it will reliquefy as soon as it comes to room temperature!)

✳ You could also transfer the eggplant to an airtight container (or multiple jars) and store in the fridge for up to a couple weeks (not that they will last that long).

The Best Tomato
BRUSCHETTA

This dish, more than any other, makes the most appearances on my table, and that's because of a few things: I can always rely on there being some stale leftover bread in my kitchen; I can always get juicy, ripe tomatoes from my garden in the summer (a must for me—but in-season store-bought are fine); and everyone loves it. Tomato bruschetta is also one of the easiest, most cost-effective and delicious dishes you can make; plus, it goes with everything. If you want to all but guarantee rave reviews, make this and serve with a glass of wine (or, even better, Peaches in Wine, page 67) for the perfect starter, or with a side of burrata or buffalo mozzarella for a complete meal.

❋ Halve the tomatoes and squeeze out and discard the seeds from half of the tomatoes. (This might sound odd, but it makes for a less watery bruschetta topping.) Dice the tomatoes and transfer to a shallow medium bowl.

❋ Add the oil, capers, garlic, oregano, basil, and a good pinch of salt. Stir and set aside while you char the bread.

❋ Heap the tomato mixture onto the bread. If desired, serve with burrata or mozzarella.

1½ pounds tomatoes on the vine

5 tablespoons extra-virgin olive oil

1½ tablespoons capers, rinsed, drained, and roughly chopped

2 garlic cloves, smashed and peeled

2 teaspoons dried Italian oregano

4 fresh basil leaves, roughly torn

Kosher salt

Charred Bread (recipe follows), for serving

Burrata or buffalo mozzarella, for serving (optional)

Recipe continues

Charred Bread

Leftover rustic Italian bread, cut into slices ½ inch thick

1 garlic clove, peeled

Extra-virgin olive oil (the good stuff), as needed (see Note)

Kosher salt

Leftover crusty bread that's been slathered in olive oil and grilled, griddled, or broiled until *this close* to being burnt might as well be considered a pantry staple in an Italian kitchen. It's not only a delicious way to use up bread that's past its prime—which is nearly a sin to waste—but when served alongside just about any dish (grilled veggies, grilled seafood, just some simple prosciutto and mozzarella, *anything*), it also becomes a complete meal.

In a tostapane (see page 20), grill pan, or under the broiler (just be sure not to set the bread on fire!), toast the bread on both sides until it's deeply browned and partially charred. Rub one side of each slice with the garlic before drizzling with olive oil and a sprinkle of salt.

NOTE

I call for using extra-virgin olive oil here because this isn't the place for anything light tasting. You want that strong, assertive flavor against the char of the bread.

Cacio e Pepe ARANCINI

Rice

1½ teaspoons freshly ground black pepper

1 tablespoon unsalted butter

1 tablespoon extra-virgin olive oil

1 small yellow onion, finely minced

Kosher salt

2 garlic cloves, finely minced

1 cup Arborio rice

2½ cups low-sodium chicken stock

¼ cup freshly grated pecorino cheese

¼ cup freshly grated Parmigiano-Reggiano cheese

Arancini

1 cup all-purpose flour

Kosher salt

3 large eggs

2 tablespoons freshly grated pecorino cheese

2 cups plain bread crumbs

4 ounces fresh mozzarella cheese, diced

Canola oil, for deep-frying

Tomato sauce (optional; see Notes), for serving

Recipe continues

My uncle Tony has been a pivotal person in my life in general, but that goes double when it comes to food. He's always owned some kind of restaurant, whether it was a pizza place or an osteria, a casual spot where they serve simple street foods like arancini, which are little balls of rice stuffed with things like meat and peas and then fried. I told Uncle Tony that I didn't want to mess around with stuffing my arancini because—as you will come to learn—I can't be bothered with fussy things. That's when he told me that he'd been making his arancini with cacio e pepe, a classic combo of cheese and black pepper, and that they'd been selling like crazy. So, I did just that, and they turned out creamy and peppery and golden brown with that cheese pull that gets you every time—exactly what arancini dreams are made of.

✻ *Cook the rice:* In a small dry skillet (not nonstick), toast the black pepper over low heat, stirring often, until fragrant, about 1 minute. Transfer to a small bowl or plate and set aside.

✻ In a medium saucepan, heat the butter and oil over medium heat. When the butter melts, add the onion and a small pinch of salt and cook until the onion is softened, about 5 minutes. Add the garlic and cook until fragrant, about 1 more minute.

✻ Add the rice and stock and bring to a boil. Reduce the heat to low, cover, and cook until the rice has absorbed the stock but is still slightly al dente, about 18 minutes.

✻ Stir in the pecorino, Parm, and toasted black pepper and give it all a good stir. Remove the pan from the heat and allow the rice to cool at room temperature. Transfer the rice to a container with a tight-fitting lid and refrigerate overnight, or for up to 24 hours (see Notes).

✻ *Make the arancini:* Set up a dredging station in three shallow bowls: In one bowl, stir together the flour and a pinch of salt. In a second bowl, whisk together the eggs and pecorino. Spread the bread crumbs in the third bowl.

Make the salsa di pomodoro from Pennette con Pomodoro (page 95).

Be sure to plan for chilling down your rice, which will need to be refrigerated overnight.

You could also stuff, roll, and coat the arancini the night before cooking them. Cover them in plastic wrap and refrigerate until ready to fry (no need to stick in the freezer).

❋ Using an ice cream scoop or soup spoon, scoop ¼ cup of the rice right into the palm of your hand, then add a piece of mozzarella right in the center. Mold the rice around it, then dredge the rice ball in the seasoned flour to coat well on all sides. Do the same in the egg mixture, then roll through the bread crumbs to coat. Place the dredged arancini on a plate or sheet pan and repeat with the remaining rice. Pop the arancini into the freezer for 15 minutes.

❋ Pour 4 inches canola oil into a small heavy-bottomed saucepan. (I like using a small pan because it contains heat better and wastes less oil. An electric skillet will work here, too.) Set over medium heat until it reaches 350°F on an instant-read thermometer.

❋ Line a plate with paper towels. Working in batches, carefully add a few arancini at a time to the hot oil and cook until the rice balls are deeply golden brown on all sides, about 5 minutes. Use a slotted spoon to transfer the arancini to the paper towels to drain.

❋ Serve hot, either on their own or with some simple tomato sauce on the side.

Grilled SCAMORZA

I'd say this recipe for grilled cheese is potentially the easiest in the book, but to call it a recipe is really an overstatement. It's more like magic, because somehow, after just a few minutes, a small handful of ingredients transforms into something absolutely divine. You take scamorza, a firm, smoked cow's milk cheese, wrap it in fig leaves, grill it until the cheese oozes, open the leaves, squeeze lemon over the whole thing, and spread it on charred bread (maybe with some roasted cherry tomatoes, but not necessarily). The fig leaves give the cheese a slightly nutty flavor, and the effect of opening them after they come off the grill is like unwrapping a present. I couldn't think of a better gift!

❁ Preheat a grill (my preference is charcoal, but gas will work, too) to high heat. If you don't have a grill, preheat your broiler to high with an oven rack in the top third of the oven.

❁ Lay a fig leaf shiny-side down on a work surface. Add a couple pieces of the scamorza, sprinkle with some chile (if using), and wrap the fig leaves over the cheese. Secure with kitchen twine. Repeat with the remaining fig leaves and cheese.

❁ Grill the fig leaf bundles seam-side down until they char and the cheese is oozing and melted, about 8 minutes total, using tongs to turn them over halfway through grilling. Transfer to a platter and cut the twine. Carefully open the leaves, drizzle with a bit of olive oil, followed by a squeeze of lemon. Serve with charred bread. Dig in!

3 large or 6 small fig leaves (see Note), rinsed

1 pound scamorza or smoked mozzarella, cut into slices ½ inch thick

1 Fresno chile, minced (optional, depending on whether you like a little heat)

Good extra-virgin olive oil, for drizzling

1 medium lemon, halved

Charred Bread (page 29)

NOTE

I find fig leaves at farmers' markets and Italian groceries, but you could also use grape leaves or organic lemon leaves, if you can get your hands on them. In a pinch, simply add the cheese to a small cast-iron skillet and pop it on the grill or under the broiler just until it's golden and bubbling. You could also use this skillet method with the fig leaves (or other leaves) instead of putting them on the grill.

My Favorite *Marinated* ROASTED PEPPERS

What else can I say about these except the fact that they're an essential. Put them on crusty bread with some sharp provolone or heaped over greens with salty cheese, and it's going to be the most delicious sandwich or salad you've ever had. And you'll never find bruschetta without a side of good marinated roasted peppers. They're also just flawless in every way: a touch smoky, garlicky, and sweet but a little bit vinegary (don't be afraid to use a generous hand with olive oil and an extra pinch of salt!). Keep a stash of these in the fridge at all times, and you'll never be more than a few minutes from your next meal.

✳ To roast the peppers, either place them directly over a gas burner on high (which is my preferred method) or slice them in half, remove the core and seeds, and roast them under a broiler (see Note). For either method, use tongs to turn the pepper every few minutes until all sides are well charred, about 15 minutes on a gas burner, or 3 to 4 minutes under a broiler. Transfer the charred peppers to a bowl and cover with plastic wrap or a plate. Set aside for 15 minutes.

✳ Peel the peppers by rubbing off the charred skin. I do this by the sink so I can rinse my hands as I go, but never rinse the peppers (this dilutes their flavor)! Cut the peppers in half (if you haven't already) over a medium bowl to catch the drippings. Discard the cores and seeds—but not the drippings!—and slice the peppers into thin strips.

✳ Transfer the strips to a bowl (if you saved the drippings in a bowl, just add the strips to them) along with the oil, vinegar, garlic, oregano, basil, and salt to taste. Let the mixture sit at room temperature for 10 minutes before serving. You could also store in an airtight container in the refrigerator for up to 5 days.

8 medium bell peppers (any color but green; I like all red)

¼ cup extra-virgin olive oil

1½ tablespoons red wine vinegar

2 garlic cloves, smashed and peeled

1½ teaspoons dried Italian oregano

A few fresh basil leaves, torn

Kosher salt

NOTE

You could also char the peppers on the grill over high heat for about 15 minutes.

Cauliflower FRITTERS

8 ounces cauliflower
(about ⅓ small head),
cut into bite-size florets
(about 1 cup)

2 cups all-purpose flour

2 teaspoons instant yeast

1 teaspoon sugar

1 cup warm water

1 large egg

2 teaspoons kosher salt,
plus more to taste

Vegetable or canola oil,
for frying

I knew I had to get the recipe for these right since they're my non-na's sister's favorite appetizer. Every time Zia Silvana would visit from Rome, she'd make these fritters, and every time, they were perfection—light and fluffy and airy, thanks to instant yeast, with the cauliflower flavor coming through. I don't know how many batches of these I had to test, but I finally nailed it. And after one bite, I felt like I was back in Italy, eating them as quickly as they were coming out of the fryer.

Just a heads-up: Your batter will need to rise for 2 hours in order to give the yeast time to work its light, airy magic.

✴ In a microwave-safe medium bowl, combine the cauliflower and ½ cup water. Cover with a plate and microwave for about 10 minutes, or until tender. Use a fork to smash the cauliflower into small pieces—don't completely mash until smooth. Set aside.

✴ In a large bowl, use a fork to stir together the flour, yeast, and sugar. Add the warm water and egg and mix again with a fork until thoroughly combined. Add the cauliflower and salt, stir to combine, and cover with plastic wrap. Let the mixture rest and rise somewhere warm until the dough has risen quite a bit and bubbles have formed on the surface, about 2 hours. I like to put mine in the oven with the pilot light on. If you don't have the ability to turn on your pilot light, you can leave it in the oven or microwave with the door closed.

✴ Pour 4 inches oil into a large heavy-duty saucepan. (An electric skillet will do the trick, too!) Set over medium heat and bring the oil to 350°F on an instant-read thermometer.

✴ Line a plate with paper towels. Working in batches of 4 or 5, add about 1 tablespoon of the battered cauliflower (the batter might feel loose, but I guarantee it's spot-on) to the hot oil. Cook until the fritters are lightly golden on both sides, about 4 minutes, using a slotted spoon to turn them over midway through frying. Transfer the fritters to the paper towels and immediately sprinkle them with a pinch of salt. Repeat with the remaining cauliflower and enjoy hot.

Batter

1 cup all-purpose flour

1 teaspoon instant yeast

1 teaspoon kosher salt

½ teaspoon sugar

1 large egg

1 cup warm water

Zucchini Blossoms

8 ounces fresh whole-milk ricotta cheese

¼ cup freshly grated Parmigiano-Reggiano cheese

Freshly ground black pepper

Vegetable or canola oil, for frying

1 dozen zucchini blossoms, center stem removed

1 (4-ounce) block provolone (see Notes), cut into 12 matchsticks ¼ inch thick

Kosher salt

NOTES

You can find zucchini blossoms at most farmers' markets and in some grocery stores during the summertime.

For a real Neapolitan experience, replace the provolone with an anchovy. You could also add bits of salami, prosciutto, or any other cured meats to the ricotta mixture.

Ask your deli counter person to slice off a slab of provolone so you can cut it into matchsticks at home (don't buy presliced).

Stuffed Zucchini Blossoms

Every summer, I plan my whole garden around how many zucchini flowers I can get, since it's not summer without stuffed zucchini blossoms. My grandmother, who also faithfully grew zucchini, would make flower fritters for the kids, and for the adults, she'd stuff them with ricotta and provolone. But because I've had a fifty-five-year-old Italian man's appetite since I was five, I didn't want the fritter; I wanted the stuffed blossoms—and if Nonna added anchovies to the filling, even better! Now I love making them for company, especially because of my guests' disbelief that such a delicacy could ever exist.

✳ ***Make the batter:*** In a medium bowl, whisk together the flour, yeast, salt, and sugar. Add the egg and water and stir with a fork just long enough for a batter to form. It should resemble a semithick pancake batter. Cover the bowl with plastic wrap and set aside to rest at room temperature for 45 minutes to 1 hour.

✳ ***Stuff the zucchini blossoms:*** In a small bowl, mix together the ricotta, Parm, and black pepper to taste.

✳ Pour about 2 inches of oil into a large Dutch oven and heat over medium heat to 350°F. You could also do this in an electric skillet.

✳ Stuff each blossom with about 1 tablespoon of the ricotta/Parm mixture and a provolone matchstick. I do this by gently opening the petals, then using my fingers to carefully get the stuffing into the center of the flower. You could also use a piping bag. Pinch the top of the petals back together and give them a gentle twist. (It's okay if the blossom rips a bit.)

✳ Line a plate with paper towels. Working in batches of 5 or 6, hold the stem end of each blossom and dip into the batter, letting any excess drip back into the bowl before placing it in the hot oil. Cook until golden brown, 4 to 6 minutes total, turning them over halfway through frying. Transfer the fried squash blossoms to the paper towels to drain and immediately sprinkle with salt. Serve warm.

PROSCIUTTO,
Figs & Melon

Behold, one of summer's most underrated pleasures: a platter of thinly sliced prosciutto plus the ripest possible melon and figs. No matter where you're going out to eat in Italy in the warmer months—Rome, Naples, Milan, Amalfi—everyone has this on their table. It's the perfect mix of sweet and salty, is so easy to make yet so chicly elegant, and is the quickest way to drive me to tears. (Now you know.) You could also take a cue from my nonna and pile everything on a sandwich and then cut it into big wedges.

1 medium cantaloupe, seeded and cut into 8 to 12 wedges, rinds removed

⅓ pound thinly sliced Prosciutto di Parma (or San Daniele, my favorite!)

8 ripe figs (I like Black Mission), halved lengthwise

✳ Place the cantaloupe wedges on a platter and drape a half slice of prosciutto over each wedge. Arrange the figs around the melon. Serve right away!

FRITTO MISTO

Most of the men on my dad's side of the family were fishermen—my nonno, all my uncles, all my cousins—so there was always an abundance of fresh seafood in the house. And if there was going to be a seafood feast, then there was going to be a little fritto misto to start. But my very favorite fritto misto memory is walking down the street on the Amalfi coast, eating a little paper cone filled with the freshest possible sardines and octopus that had been fried until exquisitely crispy and golden, needing nothing but a squeeze of lemon. My husband summed it up: "I wish more people had this much joy eating something out of a paper bag." You'll know what he's talking about when you tuck into a crisp, golden batch of this fresh out of the frying pan.

✢ Pour 4 inches of oil into a large heavy pot and heat over medium heat to 400°F.

✢ In a medium bowl, stir together the flour, cornstarch, semolina, baking powder, and a pinch of salt. Set aside while the oil gets up to temperature.

✢ Line a plate with paper towels. Working in about four batches, start dredging the seafood. Coat the first batch of seafood in the flour mixture, shake off any excess, and carefully drop it into the oil. Fry until golden, about 2 minutes. Transfer the seafood to the paper towels and sprinkle with salt and pepper. Repeat with the remaining seafood. Serve with the lemon wedges.

Vegetable or canola oil, for deep-frying

1 cup tipo "00" flour (see Notes)

½ cup cornstarch

3 tablespoons semolina

1 teaspoon baking powder

Kosher salt

1½ pounds fresh seafood (see Notes)

Freshly ground black pepper

Lemon wedges, for serving

NOTES

This recipe also calls for tipo "00" flour, a finely milled Italian flour that's typically used for pasta and pizza dough. I like using it here because it gives the fritters a lighter texture.

I like to use calamari with tentacles, shell-on medium shrimp (21/25 count; the legs, shells, and tail all get super crispy and can be eaten along with the juicy meat inside), cod fillets cut into 1½-inch pieces, small sardines, or whole anchovies. These will all cook in about 2 minutes; anything larger may need more time.

Whipped RICOTTA
with Honey & Pistachio

¼ cup salted roasted pistachios

16 ounces fresh whole-milk ricotta cheese

2 tablespoons extra-virgin olive oil

2 sprigs fresh thyme, leaves picked

½ small garlic clove

½ teaspoon finely grated lemon zest

Kosher salt

2 tablespoons honey

Charred Bread (page 29) or ruffled potato chips, for serving

Thinly sliced mortadella, for serving (optional)

Before there was whipped feta (or at least before there was whipped feta on social media!), there was whipped ricotta, which I think is *so much better* because it's creamier, milder, and pairs well with everything (shmeared on charred bread, with raw veg and grissini, on a sandwich with any Italian cured meats and figs)—and, objectively speaking, mine is the best because the combination of the ricotta and honey works with both sweet *and* salty pairings. Let me tell you, if you don't feel like making dinner, whip up a batch of this instead and sit on your back porch with some mortadella, charred bread, a bowl of ruffled potato chips, and an ice-cold glass of wine or an Aperol spritz. You're living your best life and don't let anyone tell you otherwise.

✳ In a food processor, pulse the pistachios until finely chopped. Transfer to a bowl and set aside.

✳ Without wiping out the food processor, add the ricotta, 1 tablespoon of the olive oil, the thyme leaves, garlic, lemon zest, and a pinch of salt. Process until thick and creamy, about 1 minute. Transfer the mixture to a shallow serving bowl.

✳ Drizzle the ricotta with the remaining 1 tablespoon olive oil and the honey and sprinkle with the chopped pistachios. Serve with charred bread. For the ultimate combo, also serve with mortadella!

TOMATO
Pie

I went to elementary school in Quarto, Italy. There was a bakery nearby, and on days where we had to stay later to rehearse the school play, instead of going home for lunch, I'd stop by the bakery for a slab of tomato pie they'd made in the wood-burning oven. It cost only 1 lira (about 50 cents), and all morning I'd be tempted by the scent of the olive-oily dough and sweet jammy tomatoes wafting from my bag. The *second* 1 p.m. rolled around, I'd dive in—it was the highlight of my day.

This is also one of those great recipes that you keep in your back pocket for when you don't feel like preparing anything elaborate. You can make and shape the dough ahead of time—always square, never round; you don't want a slice, you want a *slab*—then all that's left is slathering it in olive oil (the best money can buy), adding tomatoes (in season, or the best canned you can find if you don't can your own), and topping it off with fresh basil. It's the perfect representation of how Italians like to cook: simple, good ingredients prepared without fuss.

✳ *Make the dough:* In a stand mixer fitted with the dough hook, combine the flour, sugar, and yeast. Stir on medium speed to combine. With the machine running, stream in the warm water and 2 tablespoons of the oil. When the wet ingredients are about halfway incorporated, add the salt. Continue to knead on medium speed until the dough comes together and is smooth, 3 to 4 minutes.

✳ Lightly grease a large bowl with oil, add the dough, cover with plastic wrap, and allow it to rise somewhere warm (I stick it in the oven with the pilot light on; you could also put yours in the oven or microwave with the door shut) until it has doubled in size, about 2 hours.

✳ Add the remaining 3 tablespoons oil to a 16 × 16-inch pizza pan or other similar size metal or cast-iron pan (cast iron is best for a nice, crisp bottom). Deflate the dough by punching it down, then place the dough into the oiled pan. Use your hands to stretch and flatten the dough to fit the pan, flipping it over so that both sides of the dough are evenly oiled. Cover the dough with plastic wrap and allow it to rest for another 45 minutes in a warm spot.

Dough

5 cups all-purpose flour

1 tablespoon sugar

2½ teaspoons instant yeast

1¾ cups plus 2 tablespoons warm water

5 tablespoons extra-virgin olive oil, plus more for the bowl

1 tablespoon kosher salt

Tomato Topping

1 (28-ounce) can San Marzano tomatoes

1 tablespoon extra-virgin olive oil, plus more for serving

2 garlic cloves, thinly sliced

2 teaspoons dried Italian oregano

Kosher salt

Torn fresh basil leaves, for serving

Recipe continues

✳ *While the dough rests, make the tomato topping:* Preheat the oven to 425°F. (You could also roast the tomatoes in a wood-burning oven, which is what I love to do whenever weather allows for it.)

✳ Pour the tomatoes and juices into a large bowl and use your hands to tear them into bite-size pieces. Add the oil, garlic, oregano, and a pinch of salt and stir to combine.

✳ Once the dough has rested, spread about two-thirds (about 2½ cups) of the sauce over the dough, making sure the crushed tomatoes are evenly distributed. (Save the remaining sauce for another use; store in a tightly lidded container in the refrigerator for up to 5 days or in the freezer for up to 6 months.)

✳ Pop the pie in the oven to bake until the edges are a deep golden brown, about 30 minutes. Top with an extra drizzle of olive oil and some fresh basil. Let it cool slightly before slicing and serving.

Zeppole
e Panzerotti

MAKES 24
PANZEROTTI
and
24 TO 30 ZEPPOLE
(depending on their size)

Zeppole are sublime little pockets of fried dough, while panzerotti are luscious and dense potato croquettes stuffed with cheese and salami and encased in the most beautifully crispy shell. And in Italy, especially in Naples, you won't find one of these without the other, all jumbled up in a little brown paper bag you can buy on the street. We would often stop to get a batch for a predinner snack while we walked home from the beach, or my brother would hop on his scooter to grab a couple bags if my mom was having people over. (Not to mention when we'd need a bag or two after spending a late night hanging out with friends when I would visit in the summer.) Now I make a batch whenever I have people over and I want to make them a little nibble as they settle in with a glass of wine. This recipe calls for frying the zeppole and panzerotti separately, but if the timing works better for you, you can fry them at the same time; just note the different cook times for fishing them out.

❋ *Make the panzerotti:* In a large pot, combine the potatoes with enough water to cover them by 4 inches. Bring to a boil over high heat and add a generous pinch of salt (the water should taste salty). Reduce the heat to medium-low and boil until the potatoes are tender when pierced with a knife, 45 to 60 minutes. Drain the potatoes and allow them to cool.

❋ When the potatoes are cool enough to handle, peel them. Pass the potatoes through a ricer into a medium bowl. (Or mash them by hand. Just ensure that the potatoes are completely smooth with no lumps, or the panzerotti won't hold.) Season the mashed potatoes with plenty of black pepper and a pinch of salt. (Keep in mind that the mozzarella and salami will be salty.) Add the mozzarella, salami, and parsley and mix until the mixture holds together when pinched between your fingers.

❋ Line a baking sheet with parchment paper and set aside. Form 1½-ounce balls out of the potato mixture (about the size of a golf ball). Form each ball into an oblong shape and place them on the prepared baking sheet. Cover with plastic wrap and refrigerate for 1½ hours.

Panzerotti

2 pounds russet potatoes, scrubbed and unpeeled

Kosher salt and freshly ground black pepper

4 ounces part-skim mozzarella cheese (see Notes), very finely chopped

2 ounces salami, very finely chopped

3 tablespoons very finely chopped fresh Italian parsley leaves

Zeppole

2 cups all-purpose flour

2 teaspoons instant yeast

1¼ cups warm water

2 teaspoons kosher salt

Assembly and Frying

4 cups plain bread crumbs

1 cup all-purpose flour

Vegetable or canola oil, for deep-frying

Kosher salt

Recipe continues

✳ *Meanwhile, make the zeppole:* In a large bowl, use a wooden spoon to combine the flour, yeast, and water until the dough becomes tacky. Add the salt and continue mixing until combined. The dough will be very sticky. Cover the bowl with plastic wrap and set aside to rise somewhere warm and draft free (I put it in my oven with the pilot light on, or you could put it in your oven or microwave with the door closed), until the dough has doubled in size, about 2½ hours.

✳ *Assemble the panzerotti:* After the panzerotti have chilled and while the zeppole dough proofs, set up a breading station for the panzerotti in two shallow bowls: Spread the bread crumbs in one bowl. In the second bowl, whisk together the flour and 1¼ cups water until the mixture resembles a pancake batter. Set the batter aside for 5 minutes.

✳ Coat each panzerotti in the batter, shake off any excess, and then coat them in the bread crumbs, pressing the bread crumbs into the panzerotti as you work. Repeat this entire process a second time so each panzerotti is double-coated. (My uncle Tony uses this technique so the cheese doesn't come oozing out, and now I swear by it—don't skip this step!) Return the panzerotti to the baking sheet, cover them with plastic wrap, and freeze for a minimum of 45 minutes, or chill them in the fridge for up to 24 hours.

✳ *Fry the zeppole:* When the zeppole dough has finished proofing and the panzerotti are in the freezer, get ready to start frying. Line a plate with paper towels. Pour 4 inches of vegetable oil into a large heavy-bottomed pot and heat over medium-high heat to 375°F.

✳ Working in batches of 3 or 4, use a tablespoon to scoop some of the zeppole dough and another spoon to help it into the fryer. Fry the zeppole until light golden brown all over, about 2 minutes. Transfer the zeppole to the paper towels and immediately sprinkle with salt. Continue until you've used all the batter, and be sure to give your guests full permission to grab these as they come out of the fryer, since they're best served piping hot!

✳ When the panzerotti are ready, fry them in batches of a few at a time until golden, for 3 to 4 minutes. Transfer them to the paper towels and sprinkle with salt. Serve hot.

When buying mozzarella, look for the kind that comes in the little vacuum-sealed package (often labeled "low-moisture") instead of the kind packed in liquid, because the latter can have too much moisture, which can cause your panzerotti to fall apart in the fryer.

You can also fold all kinds of add-ins into the panzerotti dough. My mom loves hers with anchovies, while I'm partial to salami and alghe di mare (fresh seaweed), which has a slightly salty flavor like the Mediterranean Sea but can be difficult to find.

You could also do what my nonna does and dip anchovy fillets into the zeppole batter and fry them.

Lastly, be sure to leave yourself enough time to freeze your panzerotti dough for at least 45 minutes (or in the fridge overnight).

MUSSELS
Gratinate

3 dozen mussels,
debearded and soaked in
cold water for 15 minutes
(see Note, page 111)

1 cup plain bread crumbs

3 tablespoons extra-
virgin olive oil

2 tablespoons freshly
grated Parmigiano-
Reggiano cheese

2 tablespoons chopped
fresh Italian parsley
leaves

2 garlic cloves, finely
minced

1 tablespoon white wine
(pinot grigio for me,
always)

Lemon wedges, for
squeezing

The first time I ever enjoyed mussels stuffed with herby, cheesey, crispy bread crumbs was when I went back to Italy in 2012 for Nonna's seventieth birthday. And let me tell you, I don't normally go for "fancy" food, but that briny, salty, crunchy bite took my breath away. Now, my uncle Tony would always say, "You'll never find mussels like the ones in Bacoli"—my grandma's hometown in Naples—and while I can't necessarily disagree, you definitely don't need mussels from Bacoli to make this easy appetizer just right.

✳ Position an oven rack in the top third of the oven and preheat the oven to 500°F.

✳ Drain the mussels and give them a good scrub. Next, open the mussels. I like to do this by placing a mussel on a kitchen towel and holding it firmly on the towel with the palm of one hand, then using the other hand to carefully insert a clam knife between the top and bottom shells and gently wiggle it all the way around the mussel until the shells pop open. Be sure to reserve any liquid from the shells; you'll want about 2 tablespoons.

✳ If this method sounds too intimidating, place the mussels in a pot large enough to fit them and place it over medium heat. Heat the pot just long enough for the mussels to open slightly, a minute at the most. You don't want them to open any more than that or you'll start to cook the mussels. Once they've loosened, you can use a clam knife to pop them open the rest of the way.

✳ Arrange the mussels on the half shell on a baking sheet and set aside.

✳ In a small bowl, stir together the bread crumbs, olive oil, Parm, parsley, garlic, white wine, and reserved mussel liquid.

✳ Top each mussel with a scant tablespoon of the filling, packing it in well with your fingers. Bake for 6 minutes. Switch the oven to broil and broil the mussels for 1 minute, or until the bread crumb topping is golden brown. Serve with lemon wedges for squeezing.

50

Beef
CARPACCIO
with Fried Capers
& Shaved Parmigiano

I grew up with a mother who never met a piece of raw meat or fish she didn't like. She had nothing against sneaking a bit of raw steak when she was cooking it, a spoonful of raw meatball mixture, a nibble of raw fish. But when I discovered beef carpaccio, which is a very good beef tenderloin that's been super thinly sliced and then pounded so paper thin that it's almost see-through, I started to see that the woman had a point. Beef carpaccio—its pure flavor and buttery texture accentuated by good olive oil, a squeeze of lemon, and salt, plus some crispy capers and shaved pecorino—is probably one of life's most delicious bites. And it couldn't be easier to make.

✳ Wrap the beef in plastic wrap and pop it in the freezer for 1 hour.

✳ Meanwhile, line a plate with paper towels. In a small saucepan, heat the oil over medium-high heat until shimmering. Add the capers and fry, occasionally shaking the pan to encourage even cooking, until they begin to blossom and crisp, about 2 minutes. It happens more quickly than you'd think, so don't walk away from the pan! Transfer the fried capers to the paper towels and set aside.

✳ When the beef is ready, unwrap it from the plastic and slice it as thinly as possible. Lay the slices on a piece of parchment paper in a single layer and top with a second sheet of parchment. Using a meat mallet (or a rolling pin or the bottom of a small pan), pound the beef so the slices are as thin as possible without shredding.

✳ Carefully lift the top piece of parchment and place a platter large enough to fit all the beef top-side down. Invert the bottom sheet of parchment with the beef on it so that the beef is now on the platter. Carefully remove the parchment.

✳ *To serve:* Top the beef with the arugula and sprinkle with the crispy capers, olive oil, lemon juice, salt to taste, plenty of black pepper, and shavings of Parm. Add anchovies, if desired, and serve immediately.

8 ounces beef tenderloin

2 tablespoons extra-virgin olive oil

2 tablespoons capers, rinsed and patted dry

For Serving

3 ounces baby arugula (about 4 cups)

¼ cup extra-virgin olive oil

Juice of ½ lemon

Kosher salt and freshly ground black pepper

Parmigiano-Reggiano cheese, for shaving

8 oil-packed anchovy fillets (optional)

Carciofi
alla Romana

¼ cup minced fresh Italian
parsley leaves

¼ cup minced fresh
mint leaves

2 garlic cloves,
finely minced

1 lemon, halved

6 small round artichokes

1 cup extra-virgin olive oil

Kosher salt

Over the years, I've prepared artichokes a few different ways—roasted, fried, steamed—but when I was in Rome most recently, I was reminded that they really know how to treat an artichoke right. They get stuffed with parsley, mint, and garlic and then simmered in water and oil, where all of that flavor infuses back into the artichokes. It can be a bit labor-intensive when it comes to cleaning the artichokes, but when all is said and done and you take a bite of the sweet, tender "heart"? You'll know it was worth it.

✳ In a small bowl, toss together the parsley, mint, and garlic. Set aside.

✳ Fill a large bowl with water and squeeze in the lemon juice. Keep the squeezed lemon halves close; you'll need them in a bit.

✳ Using a small sharp paring knife, strip off the first few layers of an artichoke's leaves until you reach the light green layers. Trim the top 2 inches off the artichoke, as well as the bottom of the stem. Use the knife to carefully peel the tough outer layer of the stem to expose the tender green part. Rub a lemon half all over the artichoke to keep it from oxidizing, then use a spoon to scoop out the center choke—the fuzzy center—and discard. Use the spoon and your fingers to gently open and separate the layers of leaves of the cleaned artichoke, then add the whole thing to the lemon water. Repeat with the remaining artichokes.

✳ Use your fingers to stuff the herb and garlic mixture as best you can between the layers of the artichokes, then place the artichokes top-side down in a pot that's just big enough to hold all of them. They should fit snugly or they will float everywhere! Pour the oil over them and add enough water (usually about 2 cups) to cover the artichokes but leave the top of the stem uncovered. Add a pinch of salt and bring to a boil over medium-high heat. Reduce the heat to medium-low, cover, and simmer until the artichokes are tender, about 30 minutes.

✳ Transfer just the artichokes to a shallow serving platter and spoon a shallow layer of the cooking liquid around them. Allow the artichokes to cool to room temperature, then pluck off petals and use your front teeth to scrape off the tender meat. Continue until you get to the tender heart and devour; you'll be as addicted to these as I am!

BAGNA CAUDA

I didn't grow up eating this dish; I stumbled upon it a good ten years ago in a magazine article about recipes from Florence. I love anchovies—in anything, on anything—so I tried this out, figuring there couldn't be anything better than them melted down into oily, garlicky oblivion and whisked with melted butter. Let me tell you, my husband was hooked, I was hooked, and it instantly became a go-to appetizer with toasted bread and raw veggies. And should you have leftovers—*should you*, I'm not guaranteeing you will—a drizzle of this lends salty umami to any roasted or grilled vegetable.

✻ In a small saucepan, combine the anchovies, oil, and garlic. Cook over low heat until the anchovies practically melt into the oil, using a wooden spoon to help them break down, about 10 minutes.

✻ Whisking constantly, add the butter to the saucepan 1 tablespoon at a time. Cook until all the butter is melted and the mixture is somewhat smooth. Give the bagna cauda one last good whisk before pouring it into a butter warmer (see Notes).

✻ Serve the bagna cauda with the vegetables and bread.

12 oil-packed anchovy fillets (see Notes)

¼ cup extra-virgin olive oil

4 garlic cloves, grated

1 stick (4 ounces) good unsalted butter (see Notes), cut into 1-tablespoon pieces

About 1 pound raw vegetables for serving, such as radishes (halved), endive leaves, fennel (sliced into wedges and layers separated), and celery (sliced into batons)

About ¼ loaf good crusty baguette, cut into 1-inch cubes, for serving

NOTES

Since this is such a simple dish, go with the best anchovies, oil, and butter you can find. This is when I reach for European butter such as Kerrygold, which is creamier, richer, and more flavorful than the sticks you typically use for baking.

This dip has to be served warm or the butter will start to solidify. I like putting it in a butter warmer, the kind that has a little candle underneath, but you could also serve it in the pan you made it in and periodically reheat it as needed.

Caponata

1½ pounds eggplant (about 2 medium), cut into 1-inch cubes

4 tablespoons extra-virgin olive oil

1 small yellow onion, finely diced

2 celery stalks, finely diced

8 Castelvetrano olives, pitted and chopped

2 tablespoons capers, rinsed and drained

2 tablespoons golden raisins

¾ cup tomato puree

2 tablespoons red wine vinegar

1 tablespoon sugar

Kosher salt

2 tablespoons chopped fresh Italian parsley

A few large fresh basil leaves, torn

Crusty bread, for serving

Ricotta salata, for serving

I was introduced to this classic dish when I visited my uncle Tony in Sicily, where he moved to be with his Sicilian wife, Margherita. Neapolitan cooking doesn't usually go big on the combination of sweet and vinegary the way Sicilian cooking does, but for these stewed eggplants, I'd have them no other way. It's all about the balanced contrast among sweet raisins, salty olives, and a bright vinegary finish. Especially when it's cold out of the fridge, there's just nothing like caponata scooped onto bread with a soft or sharp cheese, or as a side to pretty much any main dish.

✳ Preheat the oven to 450°F. Line a baking sheet with parchment paper.

✳ Spread the eggplant on the baking sheet, drizzle with 2 tablespoons of the oil, and toss to coat. Roast until the eggplant is golden brown around the edges, about 15 minutes. Set aside.

✳ In a shallow Dutch oven or large skillet, heat the remaining 2 tablespoons oil over medium heat until shimmering. Add the onion and celery and sauté until the onion turns translucent, about 5 minutes. Add the olives, capers, and raisins and cook for 3 minutes to meld the flavors.

✳ Stir in the tomato puree, vinegar, sugar, and a pinch of salt. Allow the mixture to come to a gentle simmer, then reduce the heat to low, cover, and continue simmering until the mixture is slightly thickened and the flavors have melded, 20 to 25 minutes.

✳ Stir in the eggplant, cover, and cook for 10 more minutes. Season with more salt, if needed, then fold in the parsley and basil. Serve at room temperature with crusty bread and a little ricotta salata. You can store the caponata in a sealed container in the refrigerator for up to 1 week.

BRESAOLA
with Arugula & Parmigiano

Bresaola is a cured meat like prosciutto but made from beef instead of pork and not as salty. One of the best ways to serve it as an easy appetizer—and one of Nonna's favorite preparations—is to drizzle the bresaola with lots of olive oil and top it with a mound of peppery arugula, a hit of lemon juice, and shaved Parmigiano. It's absolutely worth the trip to the Italian deli to get some bresaola, which you can also keep in your fridge to enjoy just like you would prosciutto—on Charred Bread (page 29), chopped and stirred into pasta (especially Pasta alla Nerano-ish, page 92), or chopped and tossed into salads (especially my Italian Chopped Salad, page 215).

✳ Arrange the bresaola on a small platter (I usually have it slightly overlapping so it fits on the platter) and scatter the arugula on top. Season the arugula with the salt and drizzle with the olive oil and lemon juice. Finish with some shavings of Parmigiano and serve immediately.

6 ounces thinly sliced bresaola

Handful of baby arugula

Small pinch of kosher salt

1 tablespoon extra-virgin olive oil

Juice of ½ lemon

Parmigiano-Reggiano cheese, for shaving

NOTE

My nonna loves making sandwiches stuffed with this classic combination, which is really such a great choice when you think about how the lemon juice wilts down the arugula and makes a dressing with the oil to soak into the bread.

Herby Roasted TOMATOES

1 pound cherry or grape
tomatoes, halved

8 garlic cloves,
thinly sliced

¼ cup extra-virgin
olive oil

3 sprigs fresh oregano

Small handful of fresh
basil leaves

Kosher salt

I almost didn't include this dish in the book because it's difficult to really call it a dish or even a recipe. But when my husband reminded me just how often I make these—and how unbelievably delicious they are, and what a service they provide in the middle of winter when fresh tomatoes are a distant memory—I thought, *Who am I to deprive you of herby roasted tomatoes?!* The beauty of this preparation is that it scratches the itch for deep tomato flavor with very little effort, whether you spoon these over Whipped Ricotta (page 42), heap them on toast with shaved Parm as a cold-weather bruschetta, dollop them on grilled fish or chicken, toss them whole with pasta and lots of Parmigiano-Reggiano, or blend them into a thick, rich sauce. So, without further ado: herby roasted tomatoes.

✻ Preheat the oven to 400°F.

✻ In a small roasting or baking dish, toss together the tomatoes, garlic, olive oil, oregano, and basil. Sprinkle with salt and roast undisturbed until the tomatoes are caramelized around the edges, 25 to 30 minutes. Discard the oregano stems and serve as desired.

Focaccia BARESE

Dough

2 small to medium russet potatoes

4 cups all-purpose flour

2¼ teaspoons instant yeast

1 teaspoon sugar

¼ cup extra-virgin olive oil, plus more for the bowl

1½ cups warm water

1 tablespoon kosher salt

Assembly

4 tablespoons extra-virgin olive oil

Handful of pitted black olives, such as Kalamata or Gaeta

Handful of cherry or grape tomatoes, halved

1 garlic clove, thinly sliced

1 teaspoon dried Italian oregano

Kosher salt

When Zia Mimma, my aunt and godmother, came to visit me in New Jersey, she promised that she'd teach me her beloved "Barese" focaccia recipe—meaning it originated in Bari, Italy. I went to take out what I thought were all the ingredients, and she said, "No, no. We need potatoes." "*Potatoes*?" "Potatoes." Somehow my entire life I had no idea that the secret to the fluffiest, most incredible focaccia that you get pretty much anywhere in Italy—bakeries, coffee shops, bars along with a spritz—was potato. And now it's impossible for me to make it any other way. Top this with tomatoes and olives and you have just the thing for nibbling on before dinner or using for sandwiches the next day.

✳ *Make the dough:* In a small pot, combine the potatoes with just enough water to cover. Bring to a boil over medium-high heat, reduce to a simmer, and cook until the potatoes are fork tender, about 40 minutes.

✳ Transfer the potatoes to a bowl and use a ricer to mash the potatoes. Measure out 1 cup and transfer to a stand mixer. (Throw a pat of butter and a pinch of salt in any remaining potato and enjoy a cook's treat!)

✳ Fit the stand mixer with the dough hook. Add the flour, yeast, and sugar to the riced potato. Mix for about 1 minute to just incorporate the ingredients. Add the oil and warm water and continue mixing until all of the flour has been absorbed. Add the salt and knead on medium speed until the dough comes together and begins to look smooth, about 3 minutes. The dough will be a tad sticky, but that's okay.

✳ Coat a large bowl with some olive oil and add the dough. Brush a little oil over the top of the dough, cover with plastic wrap, and allow the dough to rise in a warm place until doubled in size, about 1 hour. (I stick it in the oven with the pilot light on, but you could put it in the oven or microwave with the door closed.)

✳ *Assemble the focaccia:* Add 2 tablespoons of the oil to a 9 × 13-inch metal baking pan, using a brush to evenly coat the bottom and sides of the pan. Invert the dough directly into the pan. Add a touch of the oil to your hands and gently press the dough into the pan.

✴ Press the olives and tomatoes, cut-side down, all over the dough, followed by the garlic. Drizzle the remaining 2 tablespoons oil over the dough and season with the oregano and a pinch of salt. Cover with plastic wrap and allow the dough to rise for 30 minutes.

✴ Meanwhile, preheat the oven to 450°F.

✴ Uncover the focaccia and bake until deeply golden brown, about 20 minutes. Allow it to rest in the pan for a few minutes, then transfer it to a wire rack to cool completely—if you have that much patience. Slice and enjoy!

✴ Store leftover focaccia in a sealed container in the fridge for up to 4 days. Eat it cold or reheat it in the oven or microwave.

Classic CAPRESE

1 pound fresh mozzarella cheese (preferably buffalo), cut into slices ½ inch thick

3 to 4 tomatoes on the vine, quartered

Handful of olives, preferably Castelvetrano, pitted or unpitted

2 tablespoons extra-virgin olive oil

Kosher salt

Pinch of dried Italian oregano

Small handful of fresh basil leaves, large leaves torn and smaller leaves left whole

Especially in the summer months, this dish is pretty much always on my table—along with just about every table in Italy—as a starter or light lunch or dinner. The tomatoes get cut into big, juicy wedges and drizzled with olive oil, salt, and basil, while the mozzarella is left alone—because good, fresh buffalo mozzarella is impossible to improve upon, end of story. It's a classic pairing for a reason, and one that's hard to beat on a hot afternoon.

❋ Arrange the mozzarella slices in the center of a medium shallow bowl or platter. Scatter the tomatoes and olives around the mozzarella. Drizzle everything with the olive oil, and season with a sprinkle of salt, oregano, and basil.

66

PEACHES
in Wine

1 pound peaches

1 tablespoon sugar

1 tablespoon fresh lemon juice

1 (750 ml) bottle dry red or white wine (anything you like to drink)

You can't really have an Italian book, or even talk about an Italian dinner, without including peaches in wine. It's like our version of sweet tea or sangria, and it's pretty much always on the table at gatherings in the spring and summer. (I start around Easter, even when peaches aren't technically in season here, and keep it going until right after Labor Day.) When you're preparing Sunday dinner, the first thing you do is get your peaches marinating in wine and let them sit in the fridge. Then, if you're like my nonno, you drink the wine with your meal and have the peaches for dessert (maybe with a little Gorgonzola or nuts). My mother likes to say that when she was pregnant with me, all she wanted to eat was the peaches soaked in wine—which explains a lot, because now, when peaches are in season, you can pretty much always count on there being a batch sitting in my fridge.

✧ Slice the peaches into wedges over a medium bowl (so it catches all the sweet juices that drip from the peaches). Toss the peaches with the sugar and lemon juice and set aside for 10 minutes.

✧ Add the wine to a large pitcher, followed by the peaches and all the juices in the bowl. Cover with plastic wrap and refrigerate for at least 2 hours before serving, or up to 6 hours (which is ideal). If I'm serving white wine, I like to serve it nice and chilled, but if I'm serving red, I like to bring it to room temperature 1 hour before serving.

SPRITZ
Two Ways

Ice

3 ounces Aperol or
Campari

3 ounces Prosecco

Splash of sparkling water
(about 1 ounce)

Orange slice, for garnish

In Italy, you can't even think about a get-together without handing everyone a light, refreshing spritz (followed by wine on the table for dinner). Growing up, I'd watch my zia Mimma order her spritz at a bar, and it felt like the height of sophistication, casual and special all at the same time. Now it's one of my favorite small pleasures that takes me back to summers by the sea. In my house, our best life happens when dinnertime rolls around, my husband makes us each a spritz, puts out a little bowl of chips or Bugles, and we sit in the backyard soaking up a moment in time. It's the epitome of how Italians live.

I've included two spritz recipes here—one for Campari and one for Aperol—because I love them both equally. Campari is bitter, herbaceous, and a little floral, while Aperol is slightly sweeter with hints of citrus.

✽ Fill a glass (any glass) with ice. Add the liqueur, Prosecco, and sparkling water. Garnish with a slice of orange. Enjoy!

Quick & Easy
MAINS

* (For When *Time*
& Patience Are
Short but DINNER
Is a Priority) *

WHEN I MADE ALL THOSE *big promises* in the beginning of the book about dishes that barely take any time or effort to prepare, that don't require any sides to be a meal, and that still leave you with the feeling that someone really cares even when it's your own self cooking the darn thing—I wasn't playing around. Each and every one of these recipes is something I grew up eating and that I now make for my own family on a regular basis. It always surprises people when I say this, but in Italy, dinner is all about simplicity. Because we tend to have our biggest meal at lunchtime (the rushed desk lunch is definitely not a thing for us!), in the evening is when we reach for our one-pan or one-pot meals made with a few good ingredients. And let me tell you, as important as it is to me to put dinner on the table for my family, I also have those nights when I'm racing in the door or exhausted and don't want to have to worry about cooking too many things or dealing with too many pots (and having to clean them). The recipes in this chapter are what I reach for, and they are your permission to say, "Listen, it's a one-dish kinda deal tonight," but it's still going to be a satisfying meal that everyone will enjoy. *Maybe* you pull a baguette from the freezer (if you're like me and buy two at a time so you can always have one ready to thaw until it's as good as fresh), or *maybe* you throw together a salad (and by salad, I mean Bibb lettuce, a drizzle of olive oil, a squeeze of lemon, and salt). That's All. You. Need. Throw it together, serve it with love, done. ✳

FAGIOLI
a Zuppa
over Bread

2 (15.5-ounce) cans kidney beans or borlotti beans, drained and rinsed (see Note)

1 tomato on the vine, diced

2 celery stalks, diced

1 small yellow onion, peeled and halved through the root (root end left intact)

1½ teaspoons dried Italian oregano, crushed fine between your hands

1 tablespoon extra-virgin olive oil, plus more for serving

3 large fresh basil leaves

Kosher salt

8 slices Charred Bread (page 29), for serving

Freshly ground black pepper

NOTE

I call for canned beans here instead of making them from scratch— and I stand by that. It doesn't make any difference in the soup except save you a couple hours of hard-earned time.

Both of my grandparents came from very humble beginnings. They each had a lot of siblings (four for Nonno and three for Nonna), and it wasn't always easy to put food on the table. And so their parents relied on ingredients like potatoes, lentils, and beans, which were relatively inexpensive, could be stretched and reused over multiple meals, and left everyone feeling satisfied. But even when they grew up to run a household of their own and times got better, and going to the store to buy food was no longer such a luxury, they both still preferred peasant food. They would choose a bowl of this braised bean soup over a steak any day of the week, and we kids loved to eat it right along with them. The beauty of this recipe is that it calls for lots of dried oregano, which when cooked with the beans infuses your house with the most incredible aroma—like a warm hug from Nonna.

✳ In a heavy-bottomed medium pot, combine the beans, 8 cups water, the tomato, celery, onion, oregano, olive oil, and basil. Bring to a boil over medium-high heat, then reduce the heat to medium-low, partially cover, and simmer for 45 minutes.

✳ Remove the onion halves and use a wooden spoon to gently mash some of the beans against the side of the pot. Season with salt as needed and set aside.

✳ Place a couple pieces of charred bread—torn or whole—in the bottom of each bowl, spoon over some of the beans, top with a little drizzle of olive oil, and a couple cracks of black pepper. Serve warm.

Chicken
& *Eggplant*
CUTLETS

1¼ pounds boneless, skinless chicken breasts

1 cup all-purpose flour

Kosher salt and freshly ground black pepper

4 large eggs

¼ cup whole milk

¼ cup freshly grated Parmigiano-Reggiano cheese

2 cups plain bread crumbs

1 small Italian eggplant (see Note, page 26), cut crosswise into rounds ¼ inch thick

Extra-light olive oil, for shallow-frying

Lemon wedges, for serving

I know that making chicken and/or eggplant cutlets in the middle of a busy workweek may sound like a bit of effort, but this dish can't *not* live in this chapter because it's probably what I make the most. It's one of my daughter Mia's favorite dishes, and when my little sister, Isabella, who now lives with us, walked in that first night after a breakup and this was on the table, she knew that all was right in the world again. The same thing goes for arguments with friends and generally crummy days. It's just that much of a feel-good dish and worth every bit of a little dipping and dredging. (Plus, you can cut your cleanup in half if you invest in a little electric skillet and work outside or in the garage; see Fry Me to the Moon, page 20.)

The reason why I make both chicken and eggplant is because everyone's got their favorite. For my husband, it's the eggplant, which was the only food his grandmother ever really made and is what his dad, brothers, and cousins think about most when they remember her. So anytime there's a tractor trailer leaving from my husband's warehouse in New Jersey heading to Florida where his father lives, there's a batch of eggplant cutlets on board in honor of Grandma Rose.

❋ Lay a chicken breast between two sheets of parchment paper. Using a meat mallet, rolling pin, or small heavy pan, pound the chicken until it's ¼ inch thick. Repeat for all the breasts. Set aside.

❋ Set up a dredging station in three shallow bowls: Add the flour to one bowl and season with salt and pepper. In a second bowl, whisk together the eggs, milk, and Parm. In the third bowl, stir together the bread crumbs with a pinch each of salt and pepper.

❋ Working with one at a time, dredge a piece of the chicken in the seasoned flour to coat well. Shake off any excess, then dip in the egg mixture to coat, followed by the bread crumbs. Set on a baking sheet. Repeat the process with the eggplant. Allow the dredged chicken and eggplant to rest for 10 minutes.

✴ Set a wire rack inside a sheet pan. Pour ½ inch extra-light olive oil into a large skillet and heat over medium heat to 350°F.

✴ Working in batches (in order to not crowd the pan, which will keep the cutlets and eggplant from getting nice and crispy), add the chicken and eggplant to the hot oil and cook until everything is golden brown on both sides, about 3 minutes per side. Transfer to the rack and sprinkle with salt. Between batches, discard any oil that becomes dark brown and foamy and wipe out the pan. Heat another ½ inch oil and repeat the cooking process.

✴ Serve with some lemon wedges and dig in!

NOTE
Nothing beats a good crispy cutlet with a squeeze of lemon, but you could also enjoy these on a good piece of bread with some sharp provolone or cold in a sandwich with roasted peppers, mozzarella, and balsamic.

VEAL *Scaloppine*

My younger brother was that kid who wouldn't eat anything, *anything*, but cold mini hot dogs straight out of the fridge and dipped in mayo. I'll give you a minute to let that sink in. But somehow, my mom convinced him to try her veal scaloppine, which for a while became the new only thing he would eat. And both of us *loved* it. We ate it for weeks and weeks until my mom said, "No more; go to your grandma's house." My love for veal scallopine remains, though, so I'll often re-create my mom's dish at home. It has the most deliciously rich lemony, winey sauce and reminds me of a time when we could get my brother to eat something that wasn't a cold hot dog dipped in mayo.

❋ Working with one at a time, place a cutlet between two pieces of parchment paper. Using a meat mallet, rolling pin, or small pan, pound the meat ⅛ to ¼ inch thick. Set aside.

❋ In a shallow bowl, add the flour and season with salt and pepper. Set aside.

❋ In a large skillet (preferably one that can comfortably hold all the veal at once, otherwise you'll need to cook in batches—no big deal), combine the oil and 2 tablespoons of the butter. Heat over medium heat until the butter melts and the mixture begins to simmer, 4 to 5 minutes.

❋ Season the veal on both sides with salt and pepper, then dredge in the flour to coat well. Shake off any excess flour and add the cutlets to the pan. If your cutlets won't fit in a single layer with some space between them, you'll want to do this in batches. Cook until golden and crisp, 1 to 2 minutes per side. Transfer the cooked cutlets to a plate and set aside.

❋ To the same pan over medium heat, add the stock, wine, and lemon juice. Allow the mixture to simmer until reduced by half, 6 to 7 minutes. Return the veal to the pan along with any juices that have collected on the plate. Add the remaining 1 tablespoon butter to the side of the pan to allow it to slide in, gently swirl the pan to distribute the butter under the veal, and cook for just a few more minutes for the flavors to meld. Remove the pan from the heat.

❋ Serve sprinkled with the parsley.

1½ pounds veal cutlets (see Note)

½ cup all-purpose flour

Kosher salt and freshly ground black pepper

3 tablespoons light olive oil

3 tablespoons unsalted butter

¾ cup low-sodium chicken stock

⅓ cup dry white wine (pinot grigio for me, always)

Juice of 1 lemon

2 tablespoons chopped fresh Italian parsley

NOTE

If you aren't a fan of veal, you could use chicken or even thinly sliced sirloin here. It would all be delicious.

SPAGHETTI
Aglio e Olio
di Nonna

Kosher salt

1 pound spaghetti or
bucatini (see Note)

⅔ cup extra-virgin
olive oil

4 garlic cloves,
thinly sliced

⅔ cup pitted Kalamata or
Gaeta olives, chopped

⅔ cup golden raisins

¼ cup pine nuts

Pinch of red pepper
flakes

¼ cup finely chopped
fresh Italian parsley
leaves

NOTE

*As long as we're breaking with
tradition, I like using bucatini here because
I love how their texture works with
all the other elements, but if that
gets you hot and bothered, then stick
with spaghetti!*

At its heart, this dish is all about the simplicity of garlic and olive oil, as is traditionally intended. But Nonna, who loves the combination of sweet and salty, throws in raisins and olives, plus pine nuts and pepper flakes for crunchiness and heat. When you want to cook something in 10 minutes and make everybody happy? This is the dish. And if you're not into raisins or olives or pine nuts or all of the above, add some extra Parm and you have a traditional aglio e olio. So there.

✳ Fill a large pot with water, add a generous pinch of salt, and bring to a boil over medium-high heat. Add the pasta and cook 3 minutes less than the package directions.

✳ Meanwhile, in a large skillet, combine the oil and garlic over medium-low and cook, shaking the pan occasionally, until the garlic begins to lightly brown around the edges, about 2 minutes. Add the olives, raisins, pine nuts, and pepper flakes and stir to combine. Keep the mixture over low heat while the pasta finishes cooking.

✳ Drain the pasta in a colander and immediately add it to the skillet with the sauce along with the parsley. Give everything a toss to combine, cook for 1 minute more, and then serve.

BUCATINI
with Tuna & Bread Crumbs

My godmother Zia Mimma taught me this recipe, and it's something that we've been making together for what feels like my entire life. The preparation is simple—so simple that we were able to teach it to my stepmom, which is saying something because the woman does not cook—and isn't much more than pasta simply dressed in a fresh tomato sauce, flecked with good-quality tuna, and tossed with oily, crunchy bread crumbs. It's the ultimate comfort-food dish, especially for those nights when cooking feels like the last thing you want to do.

✳ Fill a large pot with water, add a generous pinch of salt, and bring to a boil over medium-high heat.

✳ Meanwhile, in a large skillet, combine 2 tablespoons of the olive oil and the garlic and cook over medium heat, shaking the pan occasionally, until the garlic begins to lightly brown around the edges, about 2 minutes. Add the tomatoes, olives, parsley, and basil. Stir to combine, cover, and let the sauce simmer for 15 minutes. Stir in the tuna, carefully breaking it apart with your spoon. Season with a pinch of salt and remove the pan from the heat.

✳ At this point the water should be boiling. Add the pasta and cook for 2 minutes less than the package directions.

✳ While the pasta is cooking, in a small skillet, heat the remaining 1 tablespoon oil over medium heat until shimmering. Add the panko and cook, stirring, until they brown, 2 to 3 minutes. Remove the pan from the heat.

✳ When the pasta is done, drain it in a colander and immediately transfer it to the skillet with the sauce. Toss to combine and cook over medium heat for a minute for the flavors to meld.

✳ Serve topped with the crispy bread crumbs and additional parsley.

Kosher salt

3 tablespoons extra-virgin olive oil

2 garlic cloves, smashed and peeled

1 (28-ounce) can San Marzano tomatoes, crushed by hand

½ cup (about 20) Kalamata olives, pitted and halved

A few sprigs fresh Italian parsley, finely chopped, plus more for serving

A few fresh basil leaves, torn

1 (6.7-ounce) jar good Italian tuna packed in olive oil (I like Tonnino), drained

1 pound bucatini

½ cup panko bread crumbs

FRITTATA
di Maccheroni

Kosher salt

1 pound spaghetti

6 large eggs

4 ounces salami, any type, chopped (see Note)

4 ounces prosciutto, chopped (see Note)

4 ounces sharp provolone cheese, diced (see Note)

¼ cup freshly grated Parmigiano-Reggiano cheese

Freshly ground black pepper

½ cup extra-light olive oil

NOTE

For the salami, prosciutto, and provolone, if you already have some, use whatever you have—either already sliced or chop what you need from a larger hunk. We're going for whatever's easiest and potentially on hand.

Traditionally, if you made spaghetti for dinner one night, then whatever wasn't eaten went into this crispy, cheesy pie. For us, frittata di maccheroni day was always Mondays so we could repurpose what was left over from Sunday supper. It was also THE summer lunch for all the moms to bring to the beach or the pool because it was really easy to make a big batch for us kids, throw it in the cooler, give us each a big wedge the size of our freakin' heads while we're still dripping wet, then make us wait an hour before jumping back in, because Mom said so. Now I do this for my family—leftover spaghetti or not—because this dish is always a crowd-pleaser. You can make it with any pasta, but spaghetti holds a bit better.

✳ Fill a large pot with water, add a generous pinch of salt, and bring to a boil over medium-high heat. Add the pasta and cook to al dente according to the package directions. Drain and rinse under cold water to stop it from cooking any further. Set aside.

✳ In a large bowl, whisk together the eggs. Add the salami, prosciutto, provolone, Parm, plenty of black pepper, and the cooked spaghetti and toss to combine. You want the pasta well coated in the egg mixture.

✳ Heat the olive oil in a large nonstick skillet (I use my 12-inch for this) over medium heat. When the oil shimmers, add the pasta mixture, cover, and allow it to cook for 15 minutes.

✳ To carefully flip the frittata, use a spatula to help loosen the edges, then slide the frittata onto a flat surface (I use a pizza plate) and drizzle whatever oil is in the skillet on top of the pasta. Then invert your skillet over the pasta and flip the whole thing over so the frittata is now in the pan cooked-side up. Return the pan to medium heat, partially cover, and cook for another 15 minutes. The frittata should feel firm when pressed.

✳ Line a platter with paper towels. Carefully slide the frittata onto the paper towels and allow it to sit and cool for a moment before serving.

PORK CHOPS
& Fried Peppers

From the time I was little, my uncle, Zio Rosario, worked with horses. He'd get up around 4 a.m., head out to the ranch, then come home around 4 p.m. for a late lunch. Like clockwork, he'd sit and eat half a watermelon while my nonna cooked him something. Often it was pork chops and fried peppers, because that was his favorite, and he could also take leftovers the next day shoved into a roll. When my uncle was done, my cousins and I would pick at whatever juicy bits of pork chop or garlicky caramelized peppers were left in the pan. As we got older, Nonna's pan got bigger because we all wanted to sit and eat with Zio Rosario.

✳ In a large skillet (I use my 12-inch for this), heat 2 tablespoons of the oil over medium-high heat (ideally somewhere between medium and medium-high). Once the oil shimmers, working in batches, if necessary, add the pork and sprinkle salt over the top. Cook until the bottom of each piece is seared and golden, about 2 minutes. Flip, season with salt, and cook until the second side is golden brown, another 2 to 3 minutes. Transfer the chops to a plate and set aside.

✳ Return the skillet to medium-high heat and add the remaining 2 tablespoons oil and the garlic. Sauté, shaking the pan occasionally, until the garlic turns lightly golden, about 2 minutes. Add the bell peppers and season with salt. Cook, stirring occasionally, until the peppers start to soften slightly and develop some color around the edges, about 5 minutes.

✳ Return the pork to the pan, along with any juices that have collected on the plate. Give everything a good toss to combine, then reduce the heat to medium-low, partially cover, and cook, stirring occasionally, until the pork is tender (I use a wooden spoon to see if it falls apart easily, which means it's ready) and the peppers have cooked down and caramelized, about 30 minutes. You can flip the pork during this time, but it's not necessary.

✳ Stir in the olives and basil, increase the heat to between medium and medium-high, and continue cooking, uncovered, for 10 minutes to allow the flavors to meld and the peppers to cook down a bit more. Adjust the salt to taste and dig in!

4 tablespoons extra-virgin olive oil

1¼ pounds boneless pork loin chops (3 or 4), cut into bite-size pieces

Kosher salt

4 garlic cloves, smashed and peeled

3 red bell peppers, thinly sliced

½ cup pitted Kalamata olives

Small handful of fresh basil leaves

Skillet
SAUSAGE
& Crispy Potatoes

3 tablespoons light olive oil

1½ pounds Italian sausage (6 to 8 links)

2 pounds russet potatoes, peeled and cut into 1-inch cubes

Kosher salt

2 garlic cloves, smashed and peeled

½ teaspoon red pepper flakes

¼ cup fresh Italian parsley, finely chopped

Something you need to know about me: I *love* sausage. Like love it so much my best friend gave me sausage from my favorite butcher in Philly for Valentine's Day. Give me sausage, especially Italian sausage, over a pork chop or a chicken anything any day of the week. And nothing goes better with sausage than potatoes, which is why I put them together in one pan to make the easiest, best dish. The sausage cooks off while the potatoes soak up all their drippings and get crispy on the edges but fluffy on the inside. Seriously, what's not to love?

✴ In a large nonstick skillet (I use my 12-inch for this), heat a little less than 1 tablespoon of the oil over medium heat until shimmering. Add the sausages and cook until all sides are browned, about 15 minutes, turning them every few minutes.

✴ Meanwhile, fill a medium pot halfway with water and bring to a boil over medium-high heat. Add the potatoes along with a generous pinch of salt and bring the water back to a boil. Cook the potatoes for 5 minutes, then drain and leave them in the colander until you're ready for them again.

✴ When the sausages are ready, transfer them to a plate and tent them with foil to keep them warm.

✴ Place the skillet you used to cook the sausages and any drippings left in the pan over medium heat. Add the remaining 2 tablespoons oil, the garlic, and pepper flakes. After the garlic starts to lightly brown, about 2 minutes, add the potatoes. Toss them in the oil to coat, then cook in a single layer until golden and crisp, about 15 minutes. Give them a toss every few minutes but avoid touching them too much or they won't crisp. And don't be tempted to increase the heat!

✴ Sprinkle the potatoes with a pinch of salt and the parsley, then nestle the sausages among the potatoes, drizzling over any juices that have collected on the plate. Cook everything together just to meld the flavors, about 2 minutes, and serve!

Pasta
alla Norma

1¼ pounds firm eggplant (about 2 small-medium), cut into 1-inch cubes

5 tablespoons extra-virgin olive oil

Kosher salt

1 small yellow onion, minced

2 garlic cloves, smashed and peeled

1 (28-ounce) can San Marzano tomatoes, crushed by hand

Handful of fresh basil leaves, plus more for serving

1 pound rigatoni or other medium-cut pasta of choice

4 ounces mozzarella cheese, diced

Freshly grated Parmigiano-Reggiano cheese, for serving

I like this dish not only because it reminds me of my uncle Tony (he used to make it all the time), but also because it's a phenomenal vegetarian main with absolutely no need for anything else alongside it. I've changed it up a little bit from Tony's version by adding mozzarella because I like that cheesy pull, but you could leave it out and this dish would still be seriously delicious. And I call for roasting the eggplant instead of frying it so I'm not standing over my electric skillet on a weeknight making batches and batches when I'm exhausted. Plus, I think it makes for an even lighter-feeling—though extremely satisfying—dish.

✳ Preheat the oven to 425°F.

✳ Line a sheet pan with parchment paper. Spread the eggplant over the pan and top with 3 tablespoons of the olive oil and a pinch of salt. Toss to coat. Roast undisturbed until the eggplant is golden brown, about 20 minutes.

✳ Meanwhile, fill a large pot with water, add a generous pinch of salt, and bring to a boil over medium-high heat.

✳ While the water is coming to a boil and the eggplant is roasting, in a large skillet or shallow Dutch oven, heat the remaining 2 tablespoons oil over medium heat until shimmering. Add the onion and garlic and sauté, stirring occasionally, until the onion is softened and translucent, about 5 minutes.

✳ Add the tomatoes along with ½ cup water (I like measuring the water into the empty tomato can to help pick up any sauce left in the bottom), the basil, and a pinch of salt. Stir to combine, reduce the heat to medium-low, partially cover, and simmer for 25 minutes to thicken the sauce and meld the flavors.

✳ Add the pasta to the boiling water and cook 2 minutes less than the package directions.

✳ While you cook the pasta, add the eggplant to the sauce and let it simmer until meltingly tender, 8 to 10 minutes.

❋ Using a spider or slotted spoon, transfer the pasta directly from the pot to the sauce along with ½ cup of the cooking water. Increase the heat under the sauce to medium-high to bring to a rolling simmer, give everything a good toss, and cook for just a couple minutes for the flavors to meld. Remove the pan from the heat.

❋ Stir in the mozzarella and a few more basil leaves. Serve topped with freshly grated Parm.

PASTA *alla* Nerano-ish

Kosher salt

½ cup extra-virgin olive oil

1 garlic clove, smashed and peeled

1½ pounds small zucchini (see Note), sliced into thin rounds

12 ounces spaghetti

¼ cup freshly grated Parmigiano-Reggiano cheese

¼ cup freshly grated pecorino cheese

A few fresh basil leaves, torn, for serving

NOTE
You want small zucchini for this dish because they have fewer seeds, which can make the dish bitter, and a lower water content, which can make the dish soggy.

There is a restaurant on the Amalfi coast, Lo Scoglio da Tommaso, that is internationally famous for this dish (even *before* Stanley Tucci made it extra-extra famous). What makes it so surprising is that it's nothing more than the usual suspects—al dente spaghetti, garlic, olive oil—plus a whole bunch of zucchini. And yet, it's truly one of the most delicious things I've eaten in my whole life because the zucchini practically melts into the oil to become a buttery, rich sauce. And when you add in a very respectable amount of Parm and pecorino? Heaven. There are a number of versions of this dish, but this is the easiest and the closest to the original. Whenever I make it, I just turn on my pool fountains, close my eyes, and pretend I'm eating seaside in Nerano.

✻ Fill a large pot with water, add a generous pinch of salt, and bring to a boil over medium-high heat.

✻ Meanwhile, in a large skillet, combine the oil and garlic and cook over medium heat, occasionally shaking the pan, until the garlic turns light brown at the edges, about 1 minute. Add the zucchini along with a pinch of salt and cook, stirring occasionally, until the zucchini has practically melted—not crisped!—with some browning, about 30 minutes.

✻ When there's about 10 minutes left on the zucchini, add the pasta to the boiling water and cook 3 minutes less than the package directions.

✻ Reserving ½ cup of the pasta cooking water, drain the pasta in a colander and immediately transfer it to the skillet with the zucchini. Add the pasta cooking water, toss to combine, and cook for another 2 minutes, tossing occasionally, for the flavors to meld.

✻ Sprinkle with the Parm, pecorino, and basil and serve immediately.

PENNETTE
con Pomodoro

If there's one dish you can feel really good about mastering before you move on to anything else, it's this simpler than simple tomato sauce and pasta. It's essentially just pure, sweet tomatoes preserved in their freshest form that have been briefly simmered with a kiss of garlic and basil. For me, it's like the nursery rhyme of recipes. In fact, in Italy, a baby's first solid food is pastina, and then we introduce them to this sauce—which is exactly what I did with my daughter, Mia, and now it's one of her favorite dishes. Because it's such a straightforward recipe, it's essential that you use the best possible tomatoes. For me personally, that means tomatoes that I've canned myself, which I do every summer. I learned how to do it from my nonna, who would take on the task with her neighbor down the street, alternating who hosted and who brought the peaches in wine. If that's not in the cards for you, a good-quality brand of San Marzano tomatoes (such as San Marzano or Cento) will do just fine. You're still going to get that taste of summer on a cold winter day, reminding you that sunnier days are on the horizon.

Kosher salt

2 tablespoons extra-virgin olive oil

2 garlic cloves, smashed and peeled

1 (28-ounce) can San Marzano tomatoes, crushed by hand

Small handful of fresh basil leaves

1 pound pennette pasta

Parmigiano-Reggiano cheese, for serving

✳ Fill a large pot with water, add a generous pinch of salt, and bring to a boil over medium-high heat.

✳ Meanwhile, in a medium saucepan, combine the oil and garlic and cook over medium-low heat until the garlic turns light brown around the edges, about 2 minutes. Add the tomatoes, basil, and a pinch of salt. Add ½ cup water (I like to use the tomato can so I can rinse out any juice that's left in there), reduce the heat to low, and simmer, partially covered, until the sauce thickens and deepens in color, about 30 minutes.

✳ When the sauce has about 10 minutes left, add the pasta to the boiling water and cook for 2 minutes less than the package directions. Drain and return it to the same pot. Add about two-thirds of the tomato sauce and toss to coat well, then top with the last third of sauce (the Golden Italian Ratio).

✳ Serve topped with some freshly grated Parm.

PASTA
e Cucòzz

2 tablespoons extra-virgin olive oil

2 garlic cloves, smashed and peeled

2 plum tomatoes, diced

1½ pounds sugar pumpkin or butternut squash, peeled and cut into 1-inch chunks

3 sprigs fresh Italian parsley

Kosher salt

8 ounces short-cut pasta, such as ditalini

Freshly ground black pepper

½ cup freshly grated Parmigiano-Reggiano cheese

Here's a fun fact: Italians don't eat pumpkin in sweet preparations. It took me moving to the US to learn about pumpkin pie and pumpkin spice, which was pretty mind-blowing to my twelve-year-old brain. (Although truth be told, I'm not totally onboard with the whole pumpkin spice thing; don't come for me!) No matter what, though, my heart will always belong to this rich, creamy, savory pumpkin and pasta stew, which we eat on repeat in this house the second the first official day of fall rolls around. On a chilly fall afternoon, there's just nothing like a steamy bowlful topped with obscene amounts of Parm.

✳ In a large Dutch oven or large heavy-bottomed pot, combine the olive oil and garlic and cook over medium heat. When the garlic begins to lightly brown around the edges, add the tomatoes and cook for 1 minute. Add the pumpkin, parsley, a good pinch of salt, and 8 cups water. Bring the mixture to a boil. Reduce the heat to medium-low, partially cover, and simmer until the pumpkin is very tender, about 45 minutes. You can remove and discard the parsley at this point, but I keep it in.

✳ Add the pasta to the pot and cook for 2 minutes less than the package directions. Adjust the seasoning to taste with salt and a good amount of black pepper. Stir in the Parm and enjoy.

Poached
COD SALAD
with Hard-Boiled Eggs

Poached Cod

2 cups olive oil (see Notes)

1 head garlic, halved horizontally

2 fresh bay leaves

Small handful of fresh Italian parsley

2 strips lemon zest, 2½ inches long (the length of the lemon)

1 teaspoon kosher salt

1 teaspoon freshly ground black pepper

4 cod fillets (about 6 ounces each)

Dressing

4 scallions, chopped

Handful of Castelvetrano olives, pitted and roughly torn

2 tablespoons fresh lemon juice

1 tablespoon chopped fresh Italian parsley

Kosher salt (optional)

For Serving

8 cups baby arugula

1 (15.5-ounce) can cannellini beans, drained and rinsed

4 tomatoes on the vine, quartered

4 hard-boiled eggs, quartered

As someone who works from home full-time and never likes to cook a big lunch for myself, I love a recipe that gives me extras, or that I can make extras of easily, and this is one of them. I like to think of this dish as a sort of Italian Niçoise. You've got the fatty yet flaky and light fish that marries so nicely with tomatoes, hard-boiled eggs, and beans. And once you have cooked the cod, you have all that beautiful garlic- and lemon-infused poaching oil to work with. I use some to whisk into a bright, olive-flecked vinaigrette for the salad, but I save the remainder for sautéing vegetables and seafood (try it with clams!), stirring into sauces and marinades (it's the best base for puttanesca!), or drizzling over roasted or grilled veggies. It's like the gift that keeps on giving.

✳ *Poach the cod:* In a medium saucepan, combine the oil, garlic, bay leaves, parsley, lemon zest, and salt. Bring the mixture to a slow simmer over low heat and cook for 10 minutes to infuse the oil. You don't want it to come to a boil, just barely there bubbles around the edges.

✳ Add the cod so that it is completely submerged in the oil and continue to gently simmer over low heat until the cod is opaque and begins to flake, about 10 minutes. Remove the pan from the heat and transfer the cod to a shallow bowl to cool. Reserve the poaching oil and allow it to cool, but remove the bay leaves.

✳ *Make the dressing:* Measure out ¼ cup of the cooled poaching oil and transfer to a small bowl. (To store the remaining poaching oil, see Notes.) Add the scallions, olives, lemon juice, and parsley to the poaching oil and stir to combine. Season with salt, if needed.

✳ *To serve:* Pour some of the dressing over the cod. Spread the arugula, beans, tomatoes, and eggs over a serving platter or shallow bowl. Add the cod and drizzle over a bit more of the dressing.

NOTES

You can use all light olive oil for this, but you'll get better flavor in the finished product if you use half regular and half extra-virgin—I don't take lightly the added expense of using that much extra-virgin oil!

To store the oil, allow it to cool completely before straining it in a fine-mesh sieve. (I like lining mine with coffee filters; you read that right.) Transfer the strained oil to a jar with a tight-fitting lid and refrigerate for 2 to 4 weeks.

Store any leftover fish in a sealed container in the refrigerator for up to 4 days.

RIGATONI
with Sausage & Mushrooms

Kosher salt

1 tablespoon extra-virgin olive oil

1 pound sweet or spicy Italian sausage, casings removed

10 ounces button or cremini mushrooms, stems trimmed, sliced

3 garlic cloves, thinly sliced

1 pound rigatoni

2 large eggs

½ cup freshly grated pecorino cheese, plus more to taste

Freshly ground black pepper

3 tablespoons chopped fresh Italian parsley

When I tried to re-create this Zia Mimma classic, for no reason I could figure out, it wasn't the same. The ingredients seemed so straightforward, and yet that magical feeling you get when you revisit a recipe you love just wasn't there. For years I didn't think anything of it and settled for my own version, which was serviceable—until I wrote this book. Then it was time to get to the bottom of things, and that's when my zia told me that the reason hers came out differently was because she used a *couple of eggs*. Bingo! It's almost like a carbonara, where the egg marries all the ingredients together and gives them that divine next-level creaminess. *That's* what we're going for here, and I'll never again settle for anything less.

❋ Fill a large pot with water, add a generous pinch of salt, and bring to a boil over medium-high heat.

❋ Meanwhile, in a large skillet or shallow Dutch oven (my preference for this dish), heat the oil over medium to medium-high heat (I like somewhere in the middle). When the oil shimmers, add the sausage and cook, breaking it up with a wooden spoon or spatula, until just about cooked through, 6 to 8 minutes.

❋ Add the mushrooms along with a pinch of salt and cook, stirring occasionally, until the mushrooms have cooked down, about 10 minutes. Add the garlic, cook, stirring, for 1 more minute, then reduce the heat to low while you cook the rigatoni.

❋ Add the rigatoni to the boiling water and cook for 2 minutes less than the package directions.

❋ While the pasta cooks, in a small bowl, whisk together the eggs, pecorino, and a few cracks of black pepper.

❋ Just before the rigatoni is ready, scoop out 1 cup of the starchy cooking water. Slowly whisk ½ cup of the water into the eggs to temper them. Set the egg mixture and the remaining pasta cooking water aside.

❋ Drain the rigatoni and add it to the sausage mixture. Add the egg mixture and toss to combine. Remove the pan from the heat. Add the parsley and more pecorino to taste, then toss vigorously to make sure the pasta is well coated. You could add a splash more of the reserved cooking water if you need to, but you most likely won't. Serve immediately.

Crusted Seared SWORDFISH
with Green Olive Gremolata

Gremolata

1 cup finely chopped fresh Italian parsley

4 scallions, finely chopped

½ cup pitted Castelvetrano olives, roughly chopped

¼ cup packed fresh basil leaves, finely chopped

¼ cup extra-virgin olive oil

2 tablespoons fresh lemon juice

4 oil-packed anchovy fillets (optional), finely minced

1 tablespoon capers, rinsed, drained, and roughly chopped

1 tablespoon red wine vinegar

Swordfish

¼ cup extra-virgin olive oil

2 tablespoons finely chopped fresh Italian parsley

2 garlic cloves, minced

Grated zest of ½ lemon

Kosher salt and freshly ground black pepper

2 swordfish steaks (8 ounces each)

1 cup plain bread crumbs

Neutral oil for the grill (I like grapeseed oil for this)

When my uncle Tony married a woman who taught him everything she knows about Sicilian cooking, he'd always bring back some of his new favorite recipes whenever he returned to Naples from a visit to Sicily. A few years ago, it was this dish. In Sicily, they *love* swordfish, so it was such a pleasure to learn how to really treat it right, because it truly is a great "meaty" fish with nice, mild flavor. Here it gets lightly dredged in bread crumbs before being grilled to golden, crispy perfection on the outside and flaky, moist heaven on the inside. Then it gets topped off with a bright, herbaceous gremolata. It's the most beautiful marriage—just like Uncle Tony's.

✳ *Make the gremolata:* In a medium bowl, mix together the parsley, scallions, olives, basil, oil, lemon juice, anchovies (if using), capers, and vinegar. Set aside while you work on the swordfish.

✳ *Prepare the swordfish:* In a small bowl or measuring cup, whisk together the oil, parsley, garlic, lemon zest, and a pinch each of salt and pepper.

✳ Drizzle half of the marinade into a shallow plate or platter just big enough to hold the fish in a single layer. Add the fish, then pour over the remaining marinade. Set aside while you preheat the grill, about 20 minutes.

✳ Preheat the grill to medium heat (right between medium and medium-high is the sweet spot).

✳ Dredge each piece of fish in the bread crumbs and shake off any excess. Drizzle some of the neutral oil over a couple pieces of paper towel and use tongs to oil the grill grates. Place the fish on the grill and cook until the fish is opaque and firm throughout and the bread crumbs have toasted, about 5 minutes per side. Transfer the fish to a plate and allow it to rest for 10 minutes.

✳ To serve, cut each steak in half and spoon the gremolata over the top.

NOTE

I love making this on the grill because, like anything else, it's going to have more flavor. But you could also do this in the oven or on the stovetop. To cook in the oven, set the broiler to high and position an oven rack in the center of the oven. Cook the fish on a baking sheet (lined with parchment if not using a nonstick pan) until golden brown and the fish feels firm, flipping once, about 5 minutes per side. To cook on the stovetop, add a couple tablespoons of oil to a grill pan or large skillet and cook the fish until golden brown and firm, about 4 minutes per side.

Whole *Grilled* BRANZINO

When people tell me that they could never make a whole grilled fish, I tell them, "If you can grill a burger, you can grill a fish." Even if a burger makes you a little nervous, I still have faith in you because it's simple and easy and probably one of the most satisfying things you can do if you're someone who enjoys good food. If you want to seem like a person who has their life together? Grill a whole fish. If you want to look like the epitome of culinary artistry? Grill a whole fish. It's hard to mess up, because you're keeping the whole thing intact, which is going to guarantee that it doesn't dry out. All you need are a few aromatics like lemon, rosemary, and parsley, maybe a simple salad or bread, definitely some chilled crisp white wine, and you'll be pretty stinkin' happy.

✳ *Prepare the fish:* Season the inside of the branzino with salt and pepper, then stuff each cavity with the lemon slices and herbs. Drizzle 1 tablespoon of the wine into each fish, then close the fish. Using kitchen twine, tie a few loops around each fish from head to tail to keep everything inside. Drizzle the outside with some olive oil and season well with salt and pepper. Set aside.

✳ *To finish:* Preheat the grill to high heat.

✳ Drizzle some of the neutral oil over a couple pieces of paper towel and use tongs to oil the grill grates. Gently place the fish on the grill and cook until the first side has nice, charred grill marks, about 6 minutes. Carefully flip the fish—using two spatulas is my technique of choice so the fish doesn't fall apart. Grill the fish until it feels nice and firm and the eyes turn white, another 6 to 8 minutes. At the same time, add the halved lemon to the grill, cut-side down, and grill until nice and charred, about 5 minutes. Carefully transfer the fish to a plate to rest and add the charred lemon halves.

✳ In a medium bowl, toss the arugula with the oranges, fennel, a drizzle of olive oil, and a pinch of salt. Add the salad to a platter and set aside.

Fish

2 whole branzino (1 to 1½ pounds each), scaled and cleaned (a job for any fishmonger)

Kosher salt and freshly ground black pepper

1 lemon, thinly sliced

3 sprigs fresh Italian parsley

2 sprigs fresh rosemary

2 tablespoons dry white wine (pinot grigio for me, always)

Extra-virgin olive oil, for drizzling

To Finish

Neutral oil for the grill (I like grapeseed oil for this)

1 lemon, halved

About 4 cups baby arugula

2 oranges, supremed (I like navel or will use blood orange in the winter; see Notes)

1 small fennel bulb, trimmed, halved, cored, and thinly sliced into half-moons

Extra-virgin olive oil, for drizzling

Kosher salt

Mint & Anchovy Salsa Verde (page 141), for serving

Recipe continues

To supreme the oranges, slice just enough off the top and bottom so they sit flat on a cutting board. Run your knife down the sides of each orange, making sure to remove both the peel and the white pith. Holding an orange in your hand, carefully slice between each line of white membrane. The orange supremes will slide right out!

You could also make this in a really hot (450°F) oven: 12 to 15 minutes, and it'll be exactly right every time.

❋ Now carefully fillet the fish. Start by making a small slit just below the head, then gently run the tip of your knife down the center of the fish. Run your knife down the entire back of the fish, and again down the belly. This will loosen the two fillets, which you can now gently lift off the bones. Add the fillets to the platter with the arugula and drizzle the whole thing with the grilled lemon juice. Serve the salsa verde on the side.

Grilled SHRIMP
over Cannellini Beans

My dad used to take me on weekly dates to one of our favorite Italian restaurants in Philly called Radicchio. We would order a bunch of little plates to share, but what we'd always get without fail were grilled heads-on shrimp over cannellini beans. There I'd be, fifteen years old with hot pink acrylics with the white tips thinking I was the coolest, most awesome chick, tucking into these huge, juicy shrimp and loving every minute of it. The secret is marinating the shrimp first, making sure to really get in there with all that olive oil, garlic, and lemon; getting them nice and smoky on the grill (or seared in a pan); and THEN making a buttery sauce with the leftover marinade that soaks into the beans.

✳ *Marinate the shrimp (see Notes):* Use kitchen shears to snip through each shrimp shell following the rounded back of the shrimp down its full length. Leave the shell on! Lay the shrimp on a work surface and use a sharp knife to cut a shallow slit right where you snipped with the scissors to expose the vein. Use the tip of the knife to carefully pull out the little black vein and discard.

✳ In a shallow bowl, whisk together the oil, wine, chile oil, garlic, and a pinch of salt. Add the shrimp and massage the marinade into the shrimp, making sure to really get in between the shell and meat of the shrimp. Marinate for at least 1 hour or up to 2 hours in the fridge.

✳ You can cook the shrimp on a grill or a grill pan. If grilling, preheat the grill to high heat.

✳ *Prepare the beans (see Notes):* In a small bowl, soak the shallot in the ice water for 10 minutes. Drain.

✳ In a large bowl, combine the soaked shallots, beans, celery, parsley, oil, lemon juice, and a pinch of salt. Stir to combine and set aside.

Marinated Shrimp

1½ pounds heads-on jumbo shrimp (16/20 count; see Notes)

¼ cup extra-virgin olive oil

3 tablespoons dry white wine (pinot grigio for me, always)

1 tablespoon chopped Calabrian chiles in oil or a pinch of red pepper flakes

2 garlic cloves, grated

Kosher salt

Beans

1 medium shallot, thinly sliced

1 cup ice water

2 (15.5-ounce) cans cannellini beans, drained and rinsed

2 small celery hearts, minced

2 tablespoons finely chopped fresh Italian parsley

2 tablespoons extra-virgin olive oil

Juice of ½ lemon

Kosher salt

Recipe continues

To Finish

1 tablespoon olive oil
(if pan-searing)

1 tablespoon unsalted
butter

Juice of ½ lemon

2 tablespoons finely
chopped fresh Italian
parsley

✳ *To finish:* Remove the shrimp from the marinade (don't toss the marinade!). If grilling, grill the shrimp until pink and firm to the touch (a grill basket works nicely here!), about 2 minutes per side. If pan-searing, in a large skillet, heat the olive oil over medium-high heat and sear the shrimp until firm and pink, about 2 minutes per side. Transfer the shrimp to a plate and allow them to rest while you work on the sauce.

✳ In a small saucepan, combine the reserved marinade with the butter and 3 tablespoons water. Cook over medium-high heat until reduced by half, 3 to 4 minutes. Remove from the heat and stir in the lemon juice and parsley.

✳ To serve, spread the beans on a shallow platter. Top with the grilled shrimp, drizzle with the sauce, and dig in!

NOTES

If heads-on shrimp freak you out, simply replace them with really nice, large shrimp in the shell that have been deveined.

You can skip marinating the shrimp if you're in a hurry.

You can make the bean salad the night before; it will only taste better as it sits. Just be sure to bring it to room temperature before serving

PACCHERI
con Frutti di Mare

1 dozen littleneck clams, soaked in cold salt water in the refrigerator for 24 hours (see Note)

1 dozen mussels, debearded and soaked in cold water for 15 minutes (see Note)

4 tablespoons extra-virgin olive oil

4 garlic cloves, smashed and peeled

Pinch of red pepper flakes

1 dozen extra jumbo shrimp (13/15 count), peeled and deveined but tails left on

½ pound squid, cut into rounds with tentacles

Kosher salt

12 ounces cherry or grape tomatoes, halved

1 pound paccheri pasta

2 tablespoons chopped fresh Italian parsley

Small handful of fresh basil leaves, torn

Even if my grandfather or uncles weren't bringing seafood in from the boats, I could still walk down the street from my nonna's house and buy the freshest fish, mussels, clams, shrimp, octopus, squid—you name it. And twenty minutes later, if that, we'd have a beautiful meal. Now that I live in New Jersey, the quickest way for me to get back to Bacoli, where my grandparents are from and where I grew up, is to make this dish. Eating the seafood and shellfish prepared so simply with garlicky tomatoes and paccheri—my favorite cut of pasta—is like a summer day by the sea. If you forced me to pick a favorite recipe from this book, something I would not do lightly, it would be this one.

✳ Drain the clams and mussels, give them a good scrub, and set aside.

✳ In a large shallow Dutch oven, combine 1 tablespoon of the oil, 2 cloves of the garlic, and the pepper flakes and cook over medium heat until the garlic begins to lightly brown, about 1 minute. Add the clams, mussels, shrimp, and calamari. Cover and cook until the clam shells and mussels open, 3 to 5 minutes. Discard any that have not opened.

✳ While the seafood cooks, fill a large pot with water, add a generous pinch of salt, and bring to a boil over medium-high heat.

✳ Using a slotted spoon, scoop the seafood into a bowl, then pour the remaining juices into a separate cup or small bowl (you should have about ¾ cup) and set aside.

✳ In the same pot, add the remaining 3 tablespoons oil and 2 cloves garlic and sauté over medium heat until the garlic begins to lightly brown, about 2 minutes. Add the tomatoes along with a small pinch of salt. Cook for 10 minutes while you cook the pasta.

✳ Add the paccheri to the boiling water and cook for 3 minutes less than the package directions.

✳ When the tomatoes have cooked for 10 minutes, add the reserved seafood broth. Cook for 5 minutes, then return the seafood to the pot and turn the heat as low as it will go.

✳ Once the pasta is ready, drain it in a colander and immediately transfer it to the sauce. Increase the heat to medium and cook for about 2 minutes for the flavors to meld.

✳ Serve sprinkled with the parsley and basil.

NOTE

Don't be tempted to skip the step of soaking the clams and mussels. This helps the shellfish "purge" any sediment or sand tucked inside their shells, which would make your dish gritty. To debeard the mussels, use your thumb and forefinger to tug out any tough fibers sticking out from the shells.

Spaghetti
alle Vongole

This dish is giving a lot of vibes—Sunday afternoon by the Amalfi Coast, summer in a bowl, and also Christmas Eve, because we Italians always have a shellfish pasta on the table. Suffice it to say, spaghetti with clams is way up there on my favorites list, especially when you consider that it calls for just a handful of ingredients. Just be sure to use the best clams you can get your hands on.

✳ Drain the clams, give them a good scrub, and set aside.

✳ Fill a large pot with water, add a generous pinch of salt, and bring to a boil over medium-high heat. Add the pasta and cook for 2 minutes less than the package directions.

✳ While the pasta is cooking, in a large shallow Dutch oven or large pan, combine the oil, garlic, and pepper flakes. Sauté over medium heat until the garlic begins to lightly brown, about 2 minutes. Add the wine and reduce by half, 2 to 3 minutes. Add the clams, cover, and cook until all the clams open, 3 to 5 minutes. Discard any that have not opened by that point. Keep the pot over the lowest heat possible until the pasta is ready.

✳ Drain the pasta in a colander and immediately transfer it to the pot with the clams to cook over medium heat for about 2 minutes, until the pasta has absorbed some of the brothy sauce. Toss in the parsley and serve.

3 dozen littleneck clams, soaked in cold salted water in the refrigerator for 24 hours (see Note, page 111)

Kosher salt

1 pound spaghetti or linguine

½ cup extra-virgin olive oil

4 garlic cloves, smashed and peeled

Pinch of red pepper flakes

½ cup dry white wine (pinot grigio for me, always)

¼ cup fresh Italian parsley, finely chopped

Spicy Clams
& MUSSELS
with Pancetta over Toast

2 dozen clams, soaked in salted water in the fridge for 24 hours (see Note, page 111)

2 dozen mussels, debearded and soaked in cold water for 15 minutes (see Note, page 111)

3 tablespoons extra-virgin olive oil

4 ounces pancetta or guanciale, diced

3 medium shallots, thinly sliced

4 garlic cloves, smashed and peeled

½ fennel bulb, trimmed, halved, cored, and thinly sliced into half-moons

Heavy pinch of red pepper flakes

8 ounces cherry or grape tomatoes, halved

Pinch of kosher salt

1½ cups dry white wine (pinot grigio for me, always)

3 tablespoons chopped fresh Italian parsley leaves

Charred Bread (page 29)

NOTE
If you happen to have leftover gremolata from your Crusted Seared Swordfish (page 102), spoon that on here, too—truly a 100 out of 100.

At my favorite Italian restaurant in Philly, I would always order their cioppino, or a rustic seafood stew. It tasted a little bit like the Mediterranean Sea, with all the brine from the shellfish, plus a salty punch from pancetta and just the right amount of heat from a pretty generous pinch of red pepper flakes. The only thing was that they'd add gnocchi, too, which in my opinion soaked up too much of the broth. So I nixed the gnocchi and now pour the whole thing over garlicky charred bread instead. It's as close to heaven as it gets.

✳ Drain the clams and mussels, give them a good scrub, and set aside.

✳ In a large heavy-bottomed pot, combine 1 tablespoon of the oil and the pancetta. Cook over medium heat until the pancetta becomes nice and crispy, 3 to 5 minutes. Use a slotted spoon to transfer the pancetta to a plate and set aside.

✳ Return the pot with the pancetta drippings to medium heat and add the remaining 2 tablespoons oil and the shallots. Cook until they start to sizzle and become fragrant, 2 to 3 minutes. Add the garlic, fennel, and pepper flakes and cook until the shallots and fennel soften, 5 to 6 minutes. Stir in the tomatoes and salt and sauté for 5 minutes to heat the sauce through and meld the flavors.

✳ Add the wine and cook until reduced by half, 1 to 2 minutes. Add half of the parsley along with the mussels, clams, and reserved crispy pancetta. Cover the pot and cook until the mussels and clams open, about 3 minutes. Remove and discard any that have not opened after that point. Sprinkle the remaining parsley over the top and remove the pot from the heat. Serve with plenty of charred bread to sop up all those juices.

SARDE ON TOAST
& Tuna Friselle

Sarde on Toast

4 slices Charred Bread
(page 29)

1 (4-ounce) tin sardines
(see Note), packed in olive
oil or brine

A handful of baby arugula

1 Fresno chile, thinly
sliced (seeded, if you
prefer less heat)

Kosher salt and freshly
ground black pepper

Extra-virgin olive oil, for
drizzling

Juice of ½ lemon

Tuna Friselle (recipe
follows), for serving

One of the things my grandfather and grandmother would do to supplement their income in the winter, when the fish market was closed, was to preserve sarde (sardines), anchovies, and other small fish in salt and sell them. So as you can imagine, we had a lot of preserved fish in the house. And on those days when my nonna didn't want to cook dinner, she would whip out a can of sarde or anchovies and put them on charred bread with thinly sliced chiles, a little olive oil, some fresh parsley, and a squeeze of lemon. Because I had the palate of a seventy-year-old Italian man, I *loved* it. My cousins, not so much. But to this day, it's a little something special that my nonna and I share. Now I'll serve it for dinner or as something munchy to enjoy before a meal when I'm having company. And I like putting it out with some tuna friselle—good-quality canned tuna on toast with a squeeze of tomato—something my mom would whip up for dinner when no one could be bothered to turn on the stove. (No complaints here!) You could make one or both and be very happy with how quickly something so delicious came together.

✳ Top each slice of bread with some sardines, arugula leaves, and chile slices. Season with salt and black pepper, drizzle with olive oil, and finish with a little squeeze of lemon juice. Serve with tuna friselle.

NOTE

Most grocery stores sell sardines and anchovies in olive oil, and many Italian shops sell them marinated in brine—either of these is the way to go if you're new to the anchovy/sarde world because they tend to be milder. Whatever you do, don't buy them packed in salt like Nonna and Nonno used to make; that's reserved for seasoned anchovy and sardine eaters who can handle that extra-strength preserved fish action.

Tuna Friselle

SERVES 4

4 medium-size friselle

1 (6.7-ounce) jar good Italian tuna packed in olive oil (I like Tonnino)

2 tomatoes on the vine, diced

Small handful of pitted Castelvetrano olives

Pinch of dried Italian oregano

Kosher salt and freshly ground black pepper

3 tablespoons extra-virgin olive oil

Friselle are essentially twice-baked Italian crackers that you can find at any Italian shop or online, and they need to be softened slightly before serving (hence the quick soak). They come in various sizes, but I prefer the medium 5-inch ones, which I think are the ideal serving size. I've made my own in the past, but they're just as good from a package. And if you can't find them, just serve this on some Charred Bread (page 29)! (But obviously don't soak it first.) You can make these toasts with all kinds of toppings, but tuna is the most common and most preferred. On fancy nights, my mamma used to also add some buffalo mozzarella bocconcini to this, and it was unbelievably good. I've also made them with grilled vegetables, summer tomatoes on their own, cooked octopus (my uncle Tony's specialty)—you really can't go wrong!

✳ Soften the friselle slightly by quickly running them under the cold tap cut-side up. They don't need much time, as they will absorb the water and soften quickly—5 seconds, max. Set aside.

✳ In a bowl, mix together the tuna, tomatoes, olives, oregano, and salt and pepper to taste. Add the olive oil and toss everything together.

✳ Divide the mixture among the friselle and serve immediately.

Sarde on Toast & Tuna Friselle ✳ *page 116*

Halibut alla Napoletana with Olives & Capers ✳ *page 120*

HALIBUT
alla Napoletana
with Olives & Capers

2 tablespoons extra-
virgin olive oil

2 garlic cloves, smashed
and peeled

¼ cup dry white wine
(pinot grigio for me,
always)

2 (14-ounce) cans cherry
tomatoes or 1 (28-ounce)
can San Marzano
tomatoes (crushed
by hand if using San
Marzano)

⅓ cup pitted Gaeta or
Kalamata olives

1 tablespoon capers,
rinsed and drained

4 halibut fillets or
portions (4 to 6 ounces
each), or another firm
fish such as cod

Kosher salt

2 tablespoons chopped
fresh Italian parsley

This is just a classic Naples dish. You've got fish, tomatoes, garlic, and capers, so you know we're talkin' *alla Napoletana*. It's simple, quick-cooking, and you're not searing the fish, so there's no oil splattering everywhere. Instead, it simmers until juicy and flaky in a beautiful sauce, which you can spoon over bread, or even better, some fregola to soak it all up.

✳ In a large shallow Dutch oven or large pan, combine the oil and garlic and sauté over medium heat until the garlic begins to lightly brown, about 2 minutes. Add the wine and reduce for 1 minute. Add the tomatoes, olives, and capers. Partially cover the pot and simmer for 20 minutes to thicken the sauce a bit.

✳ Add the fish and cook, uncovered, until the flesh is firm, about 6 minutes. Season the sauce to taste with salt and finish with parsley.

Rice & Tuna SALAD

This is one of the dishes I've eaten most in my life, and it continues to be something you can frequently find in my fridge. It's basically summertime in a bowl, with the tomatoes, flakes of tuna, sunshine-yellow hard-boiled eggs, and corn (yes, canned because for some reason it works best that way!) tossed so simply with rice and good olive oil. But the real beauty of this salad is that it gets better the longer it sits, which is why I'm always sure to make enough to last for a couple of days.

❋ Fill a large pot with water and bring to a boil over medium-high heat. Add the rice, along with a generous pinch of salt, reduce to a simmer, and cook according to the package directions (usually about 20 minutes). When there are 10 minutes left on the timer, add the whole eggs (still in the shell) and carrots and continue cooking all together.

❋ Meanwhile, set up a medium bowl of ice and water.

❋ When the eggs are done, scoop them out of the pan and transfer to the ice bath. Drain the rice and the carrots and rinse under cold water to stop the cooking process. Set aside to drain. When the eggs have cooled, peel and chop them.

❋ In a large bowl, combine the corn, tomatoes, tuna, olives, parsley, and olive oil with a pinch of salt. Add the rice mixture and chopped eggs and mix well to combine. Add more salt to taste, if needed.

❋ Serve right away over a bed of greens or refrigerate and serve later. This will keep in a covered container in the fridge for up to 3 days.

1 cup Arborio rice (see Notes)

Kosher salt

3 large eggs

2 medium carrots, peeled and diced (see Notes)

1 (15-ounce) can corn kernels, drained

2 plum tomatoes, diced

1 (6.7-ounce) jar good Italian tuna packed in olive oil (I like Tonnino), drained and flaked with a fork

About 15 Castelvetrano olives, pitted

¼ cup fresh Italian parsley, finely chopped

¼ cup extra-virgin olive oil

Mixed greens or Bibb lettuce (my favorite), for serving

NOTES

You could use potatoes or a small pasta like bow ties instead of the Arborio rice. Add a tangy edge by adding preserved pickled eggplant.

Or feel free to add some chopped green beans and/or zucchini with the carrots for added bulk, color, and getting your veggies in.

POLLO Agrodolce

2 tablespoons light olive oil

4 bone-in, skin-on chicken thighs

Kosher salt and freshly ground black pepper

2 bell peppers (I use 1 red and 1 yellow), cut into large chunks

4 medium shallots, halved and peeled

1 Fresno chile, seeded and sliced, or a pinch of red pepper flakes

A handful of cherry tomatoes, halved

¾ cup low-sodium chicken stock

2 tablespoons honey

2 tablespoons balsamic vinegar

1 tablespoon red wine vinegar

4 or 5 fresh basil leaves, torn

2 tablespoons chopped fresh Italian parsley

Ever since my uncle Tony introduced me to sweet, tangy Caponata (page 58), I've been looking for more ways to bring that flavor combination into my life. Agrodolce is an Italian preparation that is exactly that (it literally translates to "sour sweet"), blending honey with vinegar to cook down into the most deliciously sticky, flavorful sauce. It's amazing for lacquering roasted chicken thighs, which you never have to worry about drying out or overcooking because dark meat brings all the juiciness to the party. It's a finger-licking good dish that we Italians like serving with a heel of bread (the best part of the loaf for scooping!) for sopping up all that saucy goodness—though a slice of good, crusty bread will do the trick, too.

✳ Preheat the oven to 375°F.

✳ In a large ovenproof skillet (I use my 12-inch here), heat the oil over medium heat. Season both sides of the chicken with salt and pepper. When the oil is shimmering, add the chicken to the pan skin-side down. Sear until the skin is deeply golden brown, 3 to 4 minutes. Remove the chicken to a plate and set aside.

✳ In the same pan, combine the bell peppers, shallots, and chile and sauté over medium heat until they develop some color and begin to soften, 5 to 7 minutes. Add the tomatoes and season everything with salt and pepper. Cook until the tomatoes have just begun to soften, about 2 minutes.

✳ While the tomatoes cook, in a small bowl or measuring cup, stir together the stock, honey, balsamic vinegar, and red wine vinegar.

✳ Add the honey/vinegar mixture to the pan, nestle the chicken among the vegetables, and add the basil. Bring the mixture to a boil, then transfer to the oven. Roast for 25 minutes, or until an instant-read thermometer inserted in the thickest part of the chicken registers 165°F.

✳ Sprinkle with parsley and enjoy!

Zuppa
di Latte

1 cup milk, your favorite
(I'm a 2% kinda girl)

1 shot of espresso
(see Notes)

Stale bread, torn into
1-inch pieces (enough to
soak up your milk)

1 tablespoon sugar

My nonno would get up at 3 a.m. to do his run on the boat, come home around 5 or 6 a.m., sleep for a few hours, have breakfast, and then go to the market to sell the fish he had caught. It was a grueling schedule, and to ensure that he didn't disturb anyone else in the house, my nonna kept a little daybed for him in the kitchen to take his midmorning rest. And one of my very favorite things to do was to curl up next to him. When it was time to get up, my nonna would bring us each a bowlful of zuppa di latte—warm milk mixed with leftover coffee and sprinkled with sugar—which we'd sop up with stale bread.

Now, the first time I made this for my husband, he looked at me like I had nineteen heads and asked why we were drinking bread milk soup. I'll give that to him, but it's a favorite preparation in any Southern Italian household. It comes from a time when you had to stretch a buck and was the best, most inexpensive way to fill a belly. Now it's a delicious morning ritual or something light to tide you over if you ate lunch a little too late or had a little too much for Sunday pranzo and don't feel like having a proper dinner, especially in the winter when it gets dark so early. To me, it's also the ultimate comfort food. If I take one sip of a bowl that I've prepared for myself, it takes me right back to Nonna's kitchen as if it were yesterday.

NOTES

Nonna would never make fresh espresso for zuppa di latte; it was always the leftovers that she would store in the little glass bottles that she saved from our fruit drinks. It's the perfect use for any coffee or espresso you have left in the bottom of the pot. If you use coffee instead of espresso, your proportions should be a little different—make it mainly coffee with a splash of milk—but the flavor will be about the same.

❅ In a small pot, bring the milk to a simmer over medium-low heat. Add the espresso and heat through, about 1 minute. Remove from the heat and set aside.

❅ Add the bread to a medium bowl. Pour the milk mixture over the top and sprinkle with sugar. Give the bread a few minutes to soak up the liquid and then eat with a spoon. Daydream about your happiest moments.

As for how to enjoy this dish, I personally like putting the bread in the bottom of a bowl and letting it soak up all the milk and coffee before eating it with a spoon. My nonna, on the other hand, likes to dunk her bread. To each her own.

An Italian
SUNDAY

* (Or *Any Day* Where
You Want to *Shimmy*
into *Nonna Mode*) *

THESE ARE THE RECIPES *I turn to on*
a weekend, or on days when I have the luxury of time. Not necessarily time
to cook and prep, but more time for food to cook; more time for something to
slowly simmer or braise all day to enhance and meld all those beautiful flavors, like the deep richness of bone marrow infusing into an osso buco or garlic and fresh rosemary scenting a slow-roasting chicken and potatoes. There's
more time to share the preparation of these dishes with my daughter, Mia,
and then more time to enjoy them, to have people over for dinner—the kind
of meal that lasts for hours and hours as we linger over dish after dish with
everything getting better the longer it sits. (But I will say, definitely hand off
washing dishes to someone else. If you're going to cook all day, don't feel like
you need to take on cleanup duty, too! It just wouldn't be right.)

These are the recipes I remember waking up to on a Sunday morning,
their aroma filling the house since my nonna had already been up for hours
tending to her Sunday sauce. (I honestly can't think of a more perfect way
to start the day.) And most important, they are the recipes that make meals
feel that much more heartfelt. Nothing is more welcoming or says love or joy
more than presenting something you put time and care into—and then making everyone feel like there's nowhere else they need to be but here. ✳

Bracioletti
IN SUGO

2 pounds top round steaks (about ⅛ inch thick)

1 cup loosely packed fresh Italian parsley, finely minced

⅓ cup golden raisins

¼ cup pine nuts

6 garlic cloves, finely minced

Parmigiano-Reggiano cheese, for shaving

Kosher salt and freshly ground black pepper

4 tablespoons extra-virgin olive oil

1 medium yellow onion, finely chopped

½ cup dry red wine (merlot for me, always)

2 (24-ounce) jars passata

7 or 8 fresh basil leaves

Potato Gnocchi (optional; page 133), for serving

In Naples, we don't make big braciole, the classic Sunday table dish that involves pounding beef thin then rolling it up with lots of Parmigiano, parsley, and garlic plus pine nuts and raisins for that irresistible sweet-salty bite. Instead, we make mini rolls that get melt-in-your-mouth tender when simmered for hours in a tomato sauce, while also transforming an otherwise simple sauce into something even more deeply flavorful and delicious. Sometimes just the bracioletti would go in the sauce, or sometimes meatballs and sausage would get tossed in, too, and then they get served with Nonna's Potato Gnocchi (page 133). I mean, they could go with anything, but in this family, that's it.

✳ Lay the steaks on a cutting board, cover with a sheet of plastic wrap, and use a meat mallet, rolling pin, or small pan to pound them until they're almost see-through (but not actually see-through or they'll fall apart). Cut each steak in half.

✳ With a short side of a piece of steak facing you, layer up some of the parsley, raisins, pine nuts, garlic, and a few shavings of Parm near the end of the meat. Roll the meat up away from you like a cigar, making sure to tuck in the sides so the filling doesn't escape. Secure each bracioletti with a toothpick or some kitchen twine (see Note), then season all over with salt and pepper. Set aside.

✳ In a large Dutch oven or large heavy pot, heat 2 tablespoons of the oil over medium-high heat. Add half of the bracioletti and sear until golden brown all over, about 2 minutes per side. Transfer to a plate and repeat with the remaining bracioletti.

✳ Once all the bracioletti have been seared, add the onion and remaining 2 tablespoons oil to the same pot over medium-high heat. Sauté until the onions have softened, about 4 minutes. Add the wine and reduce by half, 1 to 2 minutes. Stir in the passata. Add ¼ cup water to each jar and swish to pick up any remaining passata. Add that to the pot as well.

❊ Return the braciolettti to the pot, making sure they are submerged in the sauce, and add a generous pinch of salt and the basil. Bring to a boil, reduce to a low simmer, partially cover, and cook, gently stirring occasionally, for 2 hours. You're looking for the meat to be falling-apart tender and the sauce to be rich and just thick enough to cling to the braciolettti.

❊ Serve with fresh gnocchi, just like Nonna always does!

NOTE

I was in charge of helping Nonna roll the braciolettti, and one of the things that I remember most clearly is that I kept stabbing myself with toothpicks. So now I use kitchen twine to tie them instead. You can do either, but I choose to not bring myself back to those painful moments in life.

Potato GNOCCHI

SERVES 6 TO 8
(in a normal family;
4 in mine)

2 pounds russet potatoes,
scrubbed but unpeeled

2 cups all-purpose flour,
plus more for dusting

Kosher salt

Salsa di pomodoro
(page 95), warmed, or
unsalted butter

This was the first thing I remember learning how to cook when I was a little girl. I had a small wooden crate that I would stand on at the counter next to my nonna, and together we'd roll these out on Sundays. Now I do the same thing with my daughter, Mia, so I've been able to pass along just how superior these gnocchi are. They are the fluffiest little clouds of doughy, cheesy goodness. And the secret? Potato. I always said that if I were a vegetable, I'd be a potato—they're versatile and they please everybody. The same goes for these gnocchi. You could serve 'em with anything—a quick marinara (see page 95), in Nonna's Sunday Sauce (page 188), in place of pasta in Pasta alla Norma (page 90), with homemade pesto (from Fresh Pasta with Pesto Genovese, page 185), added to Brodo di Verdura (page 182), or be like Nonna and serve them with nothing but butter (okay, margarine, if we're being honest, but hey, it was delicious!) and lots of Parmigiano.

✳ In a large pot, combine the potatoes with cold water to cover by 2 inches. Bring to a boil over medium-high heat. Reduce to a simmer and cook until a sharp knife can easily slip into the potatoes, 30 to 40 minutes. Drain and allow to cool for 15 minutes.

✳ Pile the flour on a large wooden cutting board (Nonna insists that it be wood and I've never challenged her). Make a well in the center. Using a potato ricer, rice the potatoes right into the center of the flour. Add a very generous pinch of salt. Use a bench scraper or your hands to scoop the flour up and over the potatoes, mixing and kneading until the mixture forms a smooth dough. It will be dry at first—be patient! If the dough gets too tacky, you can add a tablespoon or two of flour until it smooths out. Place the dough in a bowl, cover with a towel, and allow it to rest at room temperature for 30 minutes.

✳ Line two sheet pans with lint-free kitchen towels, dust with flour, and set aside.

✳ Cut off a piece of dough about the size of a golf ball and use your

Recipe
continues

palms to roll it on a cutting board into a rope the thickness of your thumb. Cut the rope crosswise into ½-inch lengths. Dust the pieces with a little flour, then roll each piece over a gnocchi board or over the back of a fork ("on the hump," as Nonna would say). You want to use just enough force to create shallow grooves over the surface of the gnocchi. Add the finished gnocchi to the prepared baking sheets and continue with the remaining dough. Loosely cover with a lint-free kitchen towel and set aside to rest at room temperature for 30 minutes.

✳ Meanwhile, fill a large pot with water, add a generous pinch of salt, and bring to a boil over medium-high heat.

✳ Working in batches (I do about half of a sheet pan at a time), add the gnocchi to the boiling water. Cook until they float to the surface, 2 to 3 minutes, then use a slotted spoon or a spider to transfer them to serving bowls. I like to toss them with a little marinara to keep them from sticking together, or you could use butter instead. Repeat with the remaining gnocchi and serve as desired.

Zucchini PARMIGIANA

Sauce

2 tablespoons extra-virgin olive oil

½ small yellow onion, diced

Kosher salt

2 garlic cloves, smashed and peeled

1 (24-ounce) jar passata

4 or 5 fresh basil leaves, torn

Zucchini

1½ pounds zucchini, the smaller the better (3 or 4)

Kosher salt

1 cup all-purpose flour

3 large eggs

3 tablespoons freshly grated Parmigiano-Reggiano cheese

2 cups extra-light olive oil, or any neutral oil, such as vegetable or canola

Assembly and Serving

½ cup freshly grated Parmigiano-Reggiano cheese

1 pound pasta of your choice (optional)

Nonna would always make two Parmigianas—eggplant and zucchini. The grown-ups would have the eggplant, and the kids, who were happier with a milder, less detectable veggie, had the zucchini. It also helped that the zucchini was fried with a crisp Parm-laced crust and layered with tomato sauce and plenty more cheese. Now, whenever the summer rolls around and I have half an acre of zucchini coming in—or the markets are bursting with it—I make the zucchini Parm. It's a particularly great warm-weather lunch or dinner because it doesn't get baked. Instead, the layers of flavor slowly meld together as the dish sits at room temperature (so be sure to leave yourself about an extra hour). It also happens to make THE most delicious sandwiches the next day, which Nonna would pack for my uncles to take to work, and now I do the same thing for my husband.

✳ *Make the sauce:* In a medium saucepan, combine the oil, onion, and a pinch of salt. Sauté the onion over medium heat until softened, about 5 minutes. Add the garlic and cook until fragrant, about 1 minute. Pour in the passata, then measure ¾ cup water into the passata jar, swirl to pick up even more of the passata, and add that to the pot. Add another pinch of salt and the basil and reduce the heat to low. Cook the sauce for 25 minutes to thicken it and meld the flavors. Season with salt to taste. Remove the pan from the heat and set aside until needed.

✳ *Meanwhile, prep the zucchini:* Line a baking sheet with paper towels and set aside (but keep the roll of paper towels handy). Wash the zucchini and trim the top and bottom. With a mandoline or a sharp knife, thinly slice lengthwise into slabs about ¼ inch thick. Lay the slices in a single layer on the prepared baking sheet and lightly sprinkle them with salt (I use about a tablespoon total). Continue this process, laying down more paper towels between the layers of zucchini. Allow the zucchini to sit while the sauce cooks.

✳ When ready to cook the zucchini, spread the flour on a large plate. In a shallow bowl, whisk the eggs with the Parm.

Recipe continues

✳ Set a wire rack inside a sheet pan. In a large skillet (I use my 12-inch), heat ½ cup of the oil over medium to medium-low heat (right in between is the sweet spot) until it reaches 350°F.

✳ When the oil is ready, take a slice of zucchini and coat it in the flour. Shake off any excess, then dip it into the egg mixture to coat well. Carefully add the zucchini to the hot oil and cook until gorgeously golden brown, about 2 minutes per side.

✳ Transfer the fried zucchini to the wire rack, dab any excess oil from the top with a paper towel, and sprinkle with salt. Repeat until all of the zucchini is fried, adding more oil to the pan as needed.

✳ *Assemble:* Add a ladle of sauce to the bottom of an 8 x 11-inch 2-quart baking dish. Add a layer of zucchini and top them with a little sauce. And I mean it when I say "a little": The zucchini Parm shouldn't be swimming in sauce; it's really just there to act as a glue. I use a regular soup spoon to sauce the zucchini to avoid adding too much. Follow with a spoonful of the Parm and repeat until all of the zucchini has been used. (Not all of the sauce gets used; see next step.) Allow the zucchini to sit at room temperature for about 1 hour for the sauce to get soaked up by the zucchini and the flavors to marry completely.

✳ If desired, you can use the remaining sauce to serve with pasta. Cook the pasta for 2 minutes less than the package directions and serve with the sauce. If saving the sauce for another time, allow it to cool before storing it in an airtight container in the fridge for up to 5 days.

Grilled
SEAFOOD *with*
Mint & Anchovy Salsa Verde

While this dish could easily live in the weeknight section because it takes less than 20 minutes to prepare, I chose to include it here because it is one of the most beautiful meals you could make when you're having people over. Give me an outdoor table, a pitcher of peaches and wine, and fresh seafood going on the grill as my guests nibble on snacks, and I'll show you the ideal summertime party. Served next to a big platter of Verdura a Brace (page 216) and maybe a Whole Grilled Branzino (page 105)—seafood on seafood works!—it simply screams abundance.

❋ Preheat the grill to high heat.

❋ Season the seafood with salt and a drizzle of olive oil. Add any fish to the grill and calamari and/or shrimp to a fish grilling basket (see Note) along with the halved lemon, cut-side down. Grill until the seafood and lemon develop deep grill marks, 2 to 3 minutes. Remove the lemon and flip the seafood to repeat on the other side. You're looking for the fish to turn opaque about halfway up the fillets/steaks before flipping, after which they'll usually need an equal amount of time on the second side. The shrimp should turn a deep pink and the calamari should be opaque before flipping. Transfer everything to a plate to cool slightly.

❋ When ready to serve, arrange the arugula on a platter and top with the grilled seafood. Spoon the salsa verde over the seafood and finish with a squeeze of the grilled lemon juice.

2 pounds seafood, such as whole squid tubes (bodies) and tentacles, large shrimp (peeled and deveined), or sturdy white-fleshed fish fillets or steaks, such as swordfish or cod

Kosher salt

Extra-virgin olive oil

1 lemon, halved

Baby arugula

Mint & Anchovy Salsa Verde (recipe follows)

NOTE

The reason why I recommend having a fish grilling basket (see page 20) is because it makes cooking this dish as easy as throwing together a stir-fry. If you don't have a grill, you could also make this dish on the stovetop in a grill pan or a large skillet. If using a skillet, heat about 1 tablespoon of oil in the pan first so the seafood doesn't stick.

Recipe continues

Mint & Anchovy Salsa Verde

**MAKES ABOUT
¾ CUP**

½ bunch fresh Italian
parsley

½ cup loosely packed
fresh mint leaves

1 medium shallot, halved
and peeled

4 oil-packed anchovy
fillets

2 tablespoons capers,
rinsed and drained

2 garlic cloves, smashed
and peeled

⅓ cup extra-virgin
olive oil

Juice of 1 lemon
(about 3 tablespoons)

Kosher salt

This vibrant, pungent condiment is a staple that lives in my fridge, especially during the summer months. It helps whatever it's served with come alive, whether it's spooned over grilled fish, roasted chicken, grilled vegetables, or even just fresh mozzarella. It's also fantastic as a salad dressing.

In a food processor or mini chopper, combine the parsley, mint, shallot, anchovies, capers, and garlic and pulse until very finely chopped. Transfer to a medium bowl and stir in the oil and lemon juice. Season with salt to taste.

Polpo
alla Luciana

¼ cup extra-virgin olive oil

Pinch of red pepper flakes

4 garlic cloves, smashed, peeled, and chopped

2 pounds fresh or thawed frozen octopus (see Note)

½ cup dry white wine (pinot grigio for me, always)

8 ounces cherry tomatoes, halved

½ cup pitted Gaeta or Kalamata olives

1 tablespoon capers, rinsed and drained

1 (24-ounce) jar passata

Kosher salt

4 tablespoons chopped fresh Italian parsley

Charred Bread (page 29), for serving

NOTE

I prefer to buy frozen octopus because it's been flash-frozen at peak freshness.

I love octopus. I love it so much that I ordered it on my first date with my husband. I love it so much that even when I thought my husband was telling me I was hot but really my hair was literally on fire from the candle on the table, that still didn't keep me from eating my octopus. It's something that we enjoy in Naples pretty much any time we go out to a restaurant, whether we order it as an antipasto or on its own over bread, linguine, or risotto. And while, yes, I know that octopus can look a little intimidating to cook, it's one of the most palatable, mild, delicious, and satisfying proteins, especially when simmered in a garlic-scented tomato sauce with punches of olives and capers. It's also very forgiving because you cook it low and slow to tenderize it and help it develop flavor. Just don't set your hair on fire while doing it.

✷ In a large pot, combine the oil, pepper flakes, and half of the garlic. Sauté over medium heat until the garlic begins to lightly brown, about 2 minutes. Add the octopus and cook, flipping every now and then, until it is just beginning to curl and the ingredients have gotten to know one another, about 3 minutes. Pour in the wine and allow it to evaporate for a minute before scattering the tomatoes, olives, and capers around the edges of the pot. Cook for 5 minutes to soften the tomatoes and marry the flavors.

✷ Add the passata and remaining 2 garlic cloves. Reduce the heat to medium-low, cover, and cook until a knife slides easily into the octopus, about 45 minutes.

✷ Transfer the octopus to a shallow bowl and use kitchen shears to cut it into 2-inch pieces. (You could also do this on a cutting board with a knife.) Taste the sauce and adjust the seasoning with salt, if needed. Pour the sauce over the octopus and sprinkle with the parsley.

✷ Place the charred bread in shallow bowls and serve the octopus and sauce on top.

Roasted CHICKEN & POTATOES
with Herby Lemon Salsa

You'd never in a million years guess the secret ingredient to this roasted chicken and potato dish. It's not an Italian dish per se, nor is it something I grew up eating, but it *is* the juiciest, tenderest, and most delicious chicken I've ever had in my life. Ready for it? Anchovy paste! It gives the meat the most incredibly salty, savory depth of flavor (without any trace of fishiness), especially when it melts together with the garlic. Every household needs a recipe like this because it's so welcoming and warm and easily feeds a bunch of people. And on a chilly afternoon, when it's drizzling and gray, pop this in the oven and know that it's not going to be a wasted day after all because there's going to be roasted chicken for dinner.

✳ Preheat the oven to 400°F.

✳ *Prepare the chicken and potatoes:* In a medium bowl, combine the butter, oil, anchovy paste, garlic, lemon juice, and plenty of salt and pepper. Whisk to combine. (It will look like it won't come together at first, but it will get there.) Set aside.

✳ Lightly coat a roasting pan with oil. Lay the chicken cut-side up in the roasting pan and season the inside with salt and pepper. Flip it over so it's skin-side up and dry with paper towels. Take half of the butter mixture and smear it all over the chicken, making sure to get some under the skin, especially over the breast meat.

✳ In a large bowl, combine the potatoes with the remaining butter mixture and mix to coat well. Arrange the potatoes around the chicken along with the halved shallots and whole garlic cloves.

Chicken and Potatoes

2 tablespoons unsalted butter, at room temperature

2 tablespoons extra-virgin olive oil, plus more for the roasting pan

1 tablespoon anchovy paste (see Notes)

2 garlic cloves, grated (I like a Microplane for this)

Juice of 1 lemon

Kosher salt and freshly ground black pepper

1 whole chicken (4 to 5 pounds), spatchcocked (see Notes)

1½ pounds russet potatoes (fingerling or round baby white potatoes work, too), cut into 1-inch chunks

4 medium to large shallots, halved but not peeled

1 head garlic, cloves separated but not peeled

2 to 3 (4-inch) sprigs fresh rosemary, leaves picked

2 to 3 sprigs fresh thyme, leaves picked

Recipe continues

Herby Lemon Salsa

1 small shallot,
finely minced

¼ cup extra-virgin
olive oil

3 tablespoons chopped
fresh Italian parsley

1 tablespoon chopped
fresh chives

1 tablespoon fresh
lemon juice

1 garlic clove, minced

 Season everything one last time with salt and pepper and sprinkle with the rosemary and thyme. Roast until the chicken and potatoes are golden brown and an instant-read thermometer inserted in the thickest part of the chicken registers 165°F, about 90 minutes.

 Meanwhile, make the herby lemon salsa: In a small bowl, mix together the shallot, oil, parsley, chives, lemon juice, and garlic.

 Remove the pan from the oven, tent the chicken with foil, and let rest for 20 minutes. Carve the chicken and place on a platter with the potatoes along with the shallots and garlic. Drizzle with any juices from the roasting pan and serve with the herby salsa.

NOTES

If you have a tin of anchovies, you can make your own anchovy paste by mashing the fillets into a paste with a mortar and pestle or just a fork in a bowl. But if you'd rather just buy the paste, you can find it in most grocery stores near the canned tomatoes and tomato paste.

I typically buy my chickens already spatchcocked, which means that the backbone has been removed so the bird can lie flat. They are often sold already spatchcocked, or you can ask the butcher to do it, but it's also easy to do yourself. Place the chicken breast-side down, then use sturdy kitchen shears to cut down both sides of the backbone. (You can throw the backbone into a freezer bag and freeze until you make a batch of Brodo di Verdura, page 182, chicken broth, or other soup.) Flip the chicken over so it's cut-side down, spread the sides out onto your cutting board, and use your hands to gently but firmly press the bird flat. Done!

PIZZA
Ripiena

On Easter Monday my family would get a big bus and go on a picnic with twenty to thirty people, everyone bringing a dish to share. This is what my mom and nonna made: a sort of deep-dish "pizza" torte packed with whatever cured meat is left in the fridge, plus some eggs and ricotta. You can make it ahead of time because it only improves as it sits and is actually best at room temperature or even cold from the fridge; you can take it to the beach; and it's perfect for school lunches. The other occasion when Nonna made this would be on a holiday. She would say she just wanted a "light snack" to eat while we cooked, and the next thing I knew she'd be stuffing a pizza ripiena. She believed that unless you were sitting down and using a knife and a fork—not standing and eating with your hands, as is very appropriate with this dish—it's a snack, not a meal. All to say, you need this recipe in your life.

✳ *Make the dough:* In a stand mixer fitted with the dough hook, combine the flour, sugar, and yeast. Mix on low speed to combine. Add the water, and while kneading on low speed, sprinkle in the salt. (We do this separately to avoid potentially killing the yeast with the salt.) Increase the speed to medium and knead until the dough comes together, 3 to 5 minutes.

✳ Turn the dough out onto a clean work surface and use your hands to knead or pull the dough together, if necessary. Divide the dough into two pieces, with one piece being about two-thirds of the total dough and the other one-third size. Place the pieces of dough in a lightly oiled bowl (it's okay if they touch), cover with plastic wrap, and allow to rise somewhere warm until doubled in size, 1 to 2 hours. (I use the oven with the pilot light on. You could also just put yours in the oven or microwave with the door closed.)

Dough

3½ cups all-purpose flour, plus more for dusting

2 teaspoons sugar

2¼ teaspoons instant yeast

1⅓ cups warm water

2 teaspoons kosher salt

Oil for the bowl

Filling

8 ounces provolone cheese, chopped

1 pound salumi (I like a mix of salami, prosciutto, mortadella, and capicola, but you can use them in any combination), chopped

2 hard-boiled eggs, chopped

3 large raw eggs

½ cup fresh whole-milk ricotta cheese

Freshly ground black pepper

Olive oil, as needed

½ cup freshly grated Parmigiano-Reggiano cheese

Recipe continues

❋ *Make the filling:* In a large bowl, combine the provolone, salumi, and hard-boiled eggs. Set aside.

❋ In a medium bowl, whisk together the raw eggs and ricotta and season with plenty of pepper. Set aside.

❋ Oil the bottom and sides of a 10-inch round metal cake pan about ¾ inch deep. Lightly flour a clean work surface. Gently punch down the larger ball of dough to deflate the air and transfer it to the floured surface. Use a rolling pin to roll the dough into a 14-inch round, then carefully transfer it to the pan. Gently press the dough into the bottom and up the sides of the pan, leaving any extra hanging over the edge of the pan.

❋ Add half of the provolone/salumi mixture, then drizzle with half of the egg/ricotta mixture. Repeat with the remaining provolone/salumi mixture and remaining egg/ricotta mixture. Sprinkle the Parm over the top and set aside.

❋ Add more flour to your work surface, if necessary, and use a rolling pin to roll out the second piece of dough to a 10-inch round. Place it on top of the filling. Take the overhanging dough and pull it up and over the top edge. Seal by pinching the two pieces of dough together. Use a knife to make a small, roughly 1-inch slit in the center of the pizza, then brush the top with olive oil. Drape a clean, lint-free towel over the top and set aside to rest for 45 minutes.

❋ Preheat the oven to 400°F.

❋ Bake the pizza until deeply golden brown, 30 to 35 minutes. Allow the pizza to cool for 20 minutes before removing it from the pan and transferring it to a wire rack. Then allow the pizza to cool to room temperature (at least 30 minutes) before slicing and serving. Store any leftovers in an airtight container in the fridge for up to 5 days (but I guarantee it won't last that long).

Roasted SAUSAGE
with Grapes

We have a winery in our backyard—seriously, it's our backdoor neighbor—and the owners are friends of ours, so I developed this recipe to share with them. Roasting grapes deepens their grapey flavor and sweetness, and then you get the bright sharpness from a little vinegar to balance it out, plus the fatty, smoky, porky juices from the sausages . . . it all combines to make what I like to call "jam in a pan," which is pretty much made for spooning over polenta—and Broccoli Rabe (page 194), and Fregola with Herbs & Pine Nuts (page 224), oh my! Between the complex flavors and seriously beautiful presentation, it's one of those impressive dishes that company always loves (and no one needs to know it took you only a handful of minutes to throw together).

✳ Preheat the oven to 425°F.

✳ In a small measuring cup, whisk together the oil, balsamic vinegar, red wine vinegar, a good pinch of salt, and a few cracks of pepper. Set aside.

✳ In a 9 × 13-inch baking pan, add just enough oil to lightly coat the bottom. Add the sausages, sprinkle with the onion, and scatter the grapes around the sausages. Drizzle with the vinegar mixture and scatter the rosemary on top.

✳ Roast until the sausages have browned on the top and cooked through, about 45 minutes (no need to flip, but if you prefer for both sides to be browned, flip about halfway through). Remove from the oven and allow the sausages to cool slightly before serving over polenta.

2 tablespoons extra-virgin olive oil, plus more for the pan

2 tablespoons balsamic vinegar

2 tablespoons red wine vinegar

Kosher salt and freshly ground black pepper

2 pounds Italian sausage links (mild/sweet, hot, or a combination)

1 medium yellow onion, halved and thinly sliced

1½ pounds red grapes, preferably seedless (clustered with stems or stem-off; see Note)

1 (4-inch) sprig fresh rosemary, leaves picked

Creamy Polenta (optional; page 221), for serving

NOTE

Seeing as we have access to all different varieties of grapes, I've made this with pretty much any type you can think of—and it's fabulous every single time. You could use Concord, red, green, a mix; truly whatever you can find.

Melanzane
a Scarpone

4 small firm eggplants

2 slices day-old Italian bread (about 3½ ounces), chopped or torn into ½-inch pieces

2 plum tomatoes, diced

⅓ cup pitted Kalamata or Gaeta olives, chopped

2 ounces scamorza, smoked mozzarella, or low-moisture mozzarella, diced

¼ cup plus 3 tablespoons freshly grated Parmigiano-Reggiano cheese

¼ cup fresh Italian parsley leaves, finely chopped

2 tablespoons extra-virgin olive oil, plus more for drizzling

4 to 5 fresh basil leaves, roughly torn

2 garlic cloves, minced

1 tablespoon capers, rinsed and drained

Kosher salt

3 tablespoons plain bread crumbs

My mom's mom, Nonna Adriana, used to make us this dish all the time. She was a master of letting nothing go to waste and taught me just how tasty a piece of stale bread could be as a snack when drizzled with good olive oil and a pinch of salt—or when stuffed into eggplant with capers and olives, like I do here. As all those flavors meld together, they really do become more than the sum of their parts. This simple dish is not only supremely delicious the day it's made, but it's also really good cold.

✳ Halve the eggplants lengthwise and use a large spoon to scoop out most of the flesh. You want to leave behind just enough of the insides to create a "shell" that won't fall apart after roasting. Finely chop the eggplant flesh and add it to a large bowl.

✳ To the chopped eggplant, add the bread, tomatoes, olives, scamorza, ¼ cup of the Parm, the parsley, oil, basil, garlic, capers, and a pinch of salt. Mix well to combine and allow the mixture to sit for 10 minutes.

✳ Preheat the oven to 350°F.

✳ Place the eggplant "shells" in a roasting pan, cut-side up. Fill each half with the filling—packing it in really well. Evenly sprinkle with the bread crumbs and the remaining 3 tablespoons Parm. Give each eggplant half a drizzle of olive oil and bake until golden brown and the filling feels firm when pressed, about 1 hour. If desired, switch to broil for the last minute or so to get the bread crumbs deeply browned and crispy.

Spezzatino
with Peas

When I was living in Naples, we didn't eat red meat very often because it was a luxury. But on Sundays, Nonno would occasionally trade fresh seafood for a chuck roast, and Nonna would make a big pot of this stew. The meat simmered with the wine for hours, creating a thick, velvety broth. Now this rich and comforting beef stew is my go-to feel-good dish, which I always serve over a mound of polenta—my family's version of mashed potatoes.

❋ In a large Dutch oven or large heavy pot, heat the oil over medium-high heat.

❋ Meanwhile, add the beef to a large bowl and toss with the flour and plenty of salt and pepper until well coated.

❋ When the oil starts to shimmer, shake off any excess flour from the beef and add it to the pot in a single layer. (You may need to do this in batches.) Sear until the meat develops a deep golden brown color on all sides, 2 to 3 minutes per side. Transfer the beef to a plate and set aside.

❋ Discard all but a couple tablespoons of fat from the pot and place it over medium-low heat. Add the onion, carrots, and celery along with a small pinch of salt. Sauté, stirring occasionally, until the vegetables are tender, 5 to 7 minutes.

❋ Return the beef to the pot and add the wine, stock, parsley, and rosemary. Bring the mixture to a simmer, reduce the heat to low, cover, and cook until the sauce thickens and the meat is falling-apart tender, about 2 hours.

❋ Discard the herb stems, add the peas, and simmer, uncovered, for 20 minutes.

❋ Adjust the seasoning to taste with more salt and pepper, if needed, and serve over polenta, if desired.

¼ cup extra-light olive oil

3 pounds chuck roast, cut into 1½-inch pieces

¼ cup all-purpose flour

Kosher salt and freshly ground black pepper

1 medium yellow onion, finely chopped

2 medium carrots, peeled and finely diced

2 celery stalks, finely diced

1 cup dry white wine (pinot grigio for me, always)

1 cup low-sodium beef stock

3 sprigs fresh Italian parsley

1 (4-inch) sprig fresh rosemary

1 cup frozen peas

Creamy Polenta (optional; page 221)

NONNA'S *Proper* Pasta al Forno

Sauce

1 tablespoon extra-virgin olive oil

1 pound ground beef (I like 85% lean)

1 small yellow onion, finely chopped

½ cup dry red wine (I like merlot)

1 (24-ounce) jar passata

5 or 6 fresh basil leaves, torn

Kosher salt

Pasta al Forno

Kosher salt

1 pound rigatoni or any medium-size pasta shape of choice

Extra-light olive oil, as needed

8 ounces fresh whole-milk ricotta cheese

2 hard-boiled eggs, chopped

4 ounces salami, chopped

4 ounces provolone cheese, diced

1 pound fresh mozzarella cheese, diced or torn

½ cup freshly grated Parmigiano-Reggiano or Grana Padano cheese

Recipe continues

If Nonna was making pasta al forno (baked ziti to most Americans), then you knew something was a big deal. It's the kind of dish that calls for a little more time and attention than other pasta preparations, so it's not something she took lightly. But for a truly special occasion, like if you requested it for a birthday dinner (me, always, with a side of Broccoli Rabe, page 194), she'd treat us to this spectacular creation in which baked ziti gets the deluxe treatment with salami, provolone, and hard-boiled eggs. This is the baked ziti (or rigatoni, since I love their ridges that cling to the sauce) I put out on a Sunday when I have a table full of hungry people. Nonna's been known to make her own fresh ricotta for this (see page 42)—I don't go that far because I value my sanity, but if you want to be extra, then you'll score brownie points with her (and likely your family, too).

✳ *Make the sauce:* In a large heavy-bottomed pot or Dutch oven, heat the oil over medium-high heat (between medium and medium-high is the sweet spot). Once shimmering, add the ground beef, using a wooden spoon to break it up as it cooks. Cook until mostly browned, about 3 minutes.

✳ Add the onion and continue cooking, stirring occasionally, for another 2 to 3 minutes, until soft. Pour in the wine and allow it to reduce by half, 1 to 2 minutes. Stir in the passata. Add ¾ cup water to the empty passata jar, give it a good shake, then pour it into the pan. Stir in the basil and a pinch of salt and bring the sauce to a boil. Reduce the heat to low, cover, and simmer for 2 hours, stirring occasionally. You're looking for the sauce to be thickened and intensified in color and flavor.

✳ *Assemble the pasta al forno:* When the sauce is just about ready, fill a large pot with water, add a generous pinch of salt, and bring to a boil over medium-high heat. Add the pasta and cook 2 minutes shy of al dente. It should feel a little more underdone than you're used to, but that's what we want! Drain well and return it to the pot. Set aside.

✳ Preheat the oven to 375°F. Lightly coat a 9 × 13-inch baking dish or a 12-inch round cake pan with oil (the dish or pan should be about 2 inches deep).

✳ Add a couple ladles of the sauce to the bottom of the baking dish. Stir the ricotta and a few ladles of sauce into the pasta. Add half of the pasta to the baking dish and top evenly with the chopped eggs, the salami, provolone, half of the mozzarella, and half of the Parmigiano. Add the remaining pasta, followed by the remaining sauce, mozzarella, and Parm.

✳ Bake until golden brown and bubbling, about 30 minutes. Remove from the oven and set aside to rest for 15 minutes before serving.

Grilled
POLLO
al Mattone

On summer weekends in Italy, my brother, Sal, and I would love picking up a rotisserie chicken from the polleria, where chickens are roasted over a wood fire and occasionally misted with white wine, until the skin is crisp and golden and the meat is succulently tender and juicy. (Meanwhile, all those drippings would saturate the potatoes that roasted beneath the chickens, which is the inspiration behind Wine-Roasted Potatoes, page 205.) This heavenly preparation is not exactly the kind of thing you can get your mind off of once the craving kicks in, so I had to come up with my own version. I found that marinating a whole spatchcocked chicken in white wine and then grilling it low and slow while weighted down with a brick so the skin gets that irresistible golden crust, easily transported me back to summer Saturday nights with Sal.

✳ In a small bowl or measuring cup, whisk together the oil, wine, garlic, thyme, oregano, and parsley. Set aside.

✳ Place the chicken in a container that is big enough to hold the chicken and marinade. Season both sides really well with salt and pepper. (Use the tip of a knife to poke holes into the chicken on both sides so the marinade can really work its magic.) Pour the marinade over the chicken, cover with a tight-fitting lid, and refrigerate for 24 hours, making sure to flip the chicken halfway through.

✳ Preheat the grill to 500°F. Double-wrap two bricks or a large cast-iron skillet in foil.

✳ If using a charcoal grill, move the preheated coals to one side. If using gas, keep one section of the grill on a low flame. Drizzle some neutral oil over some paper towels and use tongs to oil the grill grates. Drain the chicken of any excess marinade and place it skin-side up on the cooler side of the grill. Place the bricks or skillet on top of the chicken, cover the grill, and cook for 30 minutes.

½ cup extra-virgin olive oil, plus more as needed

½ cup dry white wine (pinot grigio for me, always)

2 garlic cloves, grated

2 sprigs fresh thyme, leaves picked

2 sprigs fresh oregano, leaves picked and roughly chopped

Small handful of fresh Italian parsley, roughly chopped

1 whole chicken (about 4 pounds), spatchcocked (see Note, page 146)

Kosher salt and freshly ground black pepper

Neutral oil for the grill (I like grapeseed oil for this)

Lemon wedges, for serving

4 to 6 cups arugula (about 1 per person), for serving

Capers, rinsed and drained, for serving

Recipe continues

✣ Flip the chicken, put the weight back on, cover the grill, and cook for another 20 minutes.

✣ Move the chicken to the hot side of the grill, skin-side down, cover, and cook until an instant-read thermometer inserted in the thickest part of the chicken thigh reads 165°F, about 10 minutes more.

✣ Transfer the chicken to a platter and allow it to rest for 10 minutes before carving. Serve with the lemon wedges, arugula, and capers and dig in!

NOTE

*I know spatchcocking a chicken and grilling it sounds like
it could be intimidating, but trust me, if you can grill a steak (and really,
even if you can't), you can grill a whole chicken—and the payoff is grand.
That said, you could also do this in the oven. Heat a large cast-iron
skillet over medium-high heat, add about 1 tablespoon of olive oil, and place
the bird skin-side down with the bricks on top. Sear until browned
and crisp, about 4 minutes, then transfer (without flipping) to a 400°F oven
until an instant-read thermometer inserted in the thickest part of the
chicken registers 165°F, 45 minutes to 1 hour.*

OSSO BUCO
with Gremolata

Veal

8 sections of veal shank, 1½ inches long (see Notes)

Kosher salt and freshly ground black pepper

½ cup all-purpose flour

¼ cup extra-light or light olive oil

1 large yellow onion, diced

3 medium carrots, peeled and diced

2 celery stalks, diced

4 garlic cloves, minced

¼ cup tomato paste

1 cup dry red wine (I like merlot)

1 (24-ounce) jar passata

3 cups vegetable stock, plus more as needed

2 (4-inch) sprigs fresh rosemary

1 fresh bay leaf

Just the way Spezzatino with Peas (page 155) is our version of beef stew, and polenta is our mashed potatoes, this is our pot roast. Or I should really say THE pot roast, because it's better than any other you're ever going to have. The secret is using bone-in meat, which allows all that bone marrow to melt into the sauce, leaving you with the richest, most decadent gravy ever (it's a real crime to not serve this with polenta for soaking up every last bit of sauce). With a sprinkle of bright, fresh gremolata (a flavorful blend of parsley, garlic, and lemon zest) to counter all that richness, this is easily one of the best dishes in all of Italian cuisine. I make it in the fall and winter when I'm having people over and want to treat them to something special.

✳ Preheat the oven to 325°F.

✳ Tie a piece of kitchen twine around the outside of each shank to help the meat keep its shape (it should look like they're wearing a belt) and season with salt and pepper. Add the flour to a shallow dish.

✳ In a large Dutch oven or large heavy ovenproof pot with a lid, heat the oil over medium heat (between medium and medium-high is the sweet spot). Dredge the shanks through the flour to coat all sides, shaking off any excess, then add half of the shanks to the pot in a single layer. Sear until the meat is deeply golden on both sides, about 3 minutes per side. Transfer the shanks to a plate and repeat with the remaining veal.

✳ Once all the shanks are browned, add the onion, carrots, celery, garlic, and a pinch of salt to the pot. Cook, stirring often, until the veggies soften, about 10 minutes. Stir in the tomato paste and cook for 1 minute to brown it slightly. Add the wine and simmer for a couple minutes to just cook off any alcohol. Stir in the passata and stock (I like to swirl the stock in the empty passata jar first to pick up any remaining sauce). Add the rosemary and bay leaf along with the seared shanks and any juices that have collected on the plate. Make sure the shanks are submerged in the liquid.

Recipe continues

Gremolata

1 cup packed fresh Italian parsley leaves, very finely chopped

3 garlic cloves, finely minced

Grated zest of ½ lemon

Creamy Polenta (page 221), for serving (optional but strongly suggested! I make a double batch when serving 8)

❊ Bring to a boil, then cover and transfer the pot to the oven. Cook for 3 hours. Halfway through, without turning the shanks, check to see if there's still a significant amount of liquid. If there's not at least a couple of cups left, add a touch more stock.

❊ *Meanwhile, make the gremolata:* In a small bowl, combine the parsley, garlic, and lemon zest. Set aside.

❊ When the veal is done roasting, carefully transfer the shanks to a large shallow platter and snip off and discard the twine. The sauce should be nice and thick at this point, enough to cling to the meat. If not, you can boil it down on the stove until it thickens.

❊ When ready to serve, skim any fat from the surface of the sauce, adjust the seasoning with more salt, if needed, and spoon it over the veal. Sprinkle the veal with the gremolata. If desired, serve with polenta.

NOTES

I prefer to use veal shanks for this dish, but you could use beef shanks, which you can usually find in specialty markets. You will need to adjust the cook time to 4 to 6 hours, depending on their size.

This dish is best cooked the day before you're meant to serve it. I let it cool to room temperature in the pot, then store it in the fridge just like that. That way the next day it's very easy to skim off any fat that's solidified on the top of the sauce and pop it back onto the stove or into a 300°F oven to reheat for 1 hour.

Stuffed & *Braised* CALAMARI

SERVES 6 TO 8
*(about 2 stuffed calamari
per person)*

Most of my friends here in the States grew up eating the same kinds of comfort foods: burgers, casseroles, mac 'n' cheese. But my version of that simple, feel-good dish is stuffed seafood. Give me a stuffed fish or calamari and I'm very, very happy not only because it's delicious—especially when it's packed with bread crumbs, cheese, and parsley—but also because it reminds me of the ultimate celebration: Christmas Eve at my grandparents' house. Now, anyone who knows me is well aware that I have no patience for things that are fussy in any way, so it's really saying something that I love making this recipe (because yes . . . it's a *little* fussy). Stuffed calamari has become a fan favorite of my annual Christmas Eve spread, either as a second or third course or sliced thin and served as a starter on an antipasto platter. If your nonna didn't teach you how to make stuffed calamari, then let me be your nonna—I assure you, you'll never make stuffed calamari any other way.

✳ *Make the stuffing:* In a medium skillet, combine the oil and garlic and sauté over medium heat, occasionally swirling the pan, until the garlic starts to lightly brown, about 1 minute. Add the tentacles, fresh tomatoes, a small pinch of salt, and 2 tablespoons of the parsley. Cook until the tentacles are opaque and firm and the sauce has started to cook down, about 5 minutes. Remove the pan from the heat and let the tentacle mixture cool to room temperature.

✳ In a large bowl, combine the cooled tentacle mixture, the bread crumbs, provola, Parm, remaining 2 tablespoons parsley, and the egg and mix well.

Stuffing

1 tablespoon extra-virgin olive oil

1 garlic clove, minced

½ pound squid tentacles, finely chopped

½ cup fresh cherry or grape tomatoes, halved

Kosher salt

4 tablespoons chopped fresh Italian parsley

⅔ cup plain bread crumbs

½ cup diced provola or mozzarella cheese

¼ cup freshly grated Parmigiano-Reggiano cheese

1 large egg

Recipe continues

✳ *Stuff the calamari:* Transfer the stuffing to a piping bag with no tip or a zip-top plastic bag with the corner snipped off (or use a spoon and your fingers) and stuff each squid tube two-thirds full with the filling. Weave a few toothpicks through the opening of each tube to pin it closed.

✳ In a large skillet, heat the olive oil over medium heat until shimmering. Add the stuffed calamari in a single layer and sear on all sides until golden, about 6 minutes total.

✳ Add the garlic and sauté until just fragrant, about 1 minute. Pour in the wine and allow for it to reduce for 1 minute. Add the canned tomatoes, pepper flakes, and basil. Bring to a boil, reduce the heat to medium-low, partially cover the pan, and cook until the sauce is thick and the squid is firm to the touch and tender when sliced, about 1 hour. This cook time yields expertly cooked squid every time, but you'll know you're in the right territory when the squid is no longer tough and chewy. Transfer the squid to a serving plate.

✳ Season the sauce with salt to taste and serve with the squid, maybe with ridiculously big chunks of Italian bread for dipping . . . or maybe with pasta (see Notes).

Stuffed Calamari

12 to 16 medium to large squid tubes (see Notes), about 1½ pounds, rinsed

2 tablespoons extra-virgin olive oil

2 garlic cloves, minced

⅓ cup white wine (pinot grigio for me, always)

1 (28-ounce) can cherry or San Marzano tomatoes, crushed by hand

Pinch of red pepper flakes

3 or 4 fresh basil leaves, torn

Kosher salt

Crusty Italian bread or pasta, for serving (optional)

NOTES

Medium to large squid tubes are better for stuffing; get enough so there are 2 per serving.

You could serve this right out of the pot, or you could let the calamari cool, refrigerate it right in the pot overnight, and then reheat it just before serving. This allows the flavors to get to know one another, and the bread crumbs in the stuffing soak it all up.

I recommend cooking a pound of spaghetti to toss with the sauce and then serve the calamari alongside.

BISTECCA
alla Fiorentina

1 (2½-pound) bone-in
steak, 3 inches thick, such
as rib eye, New York strip,
or porterhouse steak

Kosher salt and freshly
ground black pepper

½ lemon

1 tablespoon extra-virgin
olive oil

Flaky sea salt, such as
Maldon (optional)

A few years ago, I had the privilege of spending a week in Tuscany and eating my way through the region. While it's impossible to pick just one thing that was the pinnacle of the trip, right at the top would have to be our visit to Dario Cecchini's restaurant, Antica Macelleria Cecchini, in the town of Panzano in Chianti. Dario Cecchini is a legendary butcher, and being in his presence was a true bucket-list moment. But what really made it next-level was getting to watch him prepare one of his most famous dishes, bistecca alla fiorentina, a massive steak, 3 to 4 inches thick, seasoned simply and grilled. So when he described how he likes to cook it, I wrote down everything he said (see Dario's Tips for the Perfect Bistecca alla Fiorentina, opposite). Now I make this at home on my grill with the sunset in the background, a glass of wine in hand, and all the sides I love on the table and think *Tuscany what? Tuscany who?*

✳ Remove the steak from the fridge and allow it to sit at room temperature while you get the grill ready (about 30 minutes).

✳ Preheat a grill to medium-high heat. If using a charcoal grill, push the charcoal to one side so you have indirect heat on one side and direct heat on the other. If using a gas grill, turn down the burners on one half of the grill.

✳ Generously season the steak with salt and pepper on both sides, then use your hand to gently press the seasoning into the meat.

✳ Add the steak to the cooler side of the grill and cook for 20 minutes (see Notes).

✳ Move the steak to the direct heat for 5 minutes and leave it be so it can get some nicely charred grill marks.

✳ Flip the steak over and once again place it over the indirect heat. Grill for another 20 minutes.

✳ Finish with 5 minutes over direct heat. At this point, the steak's internal temperature should read 130°F on an instant-read thermometer for medium-rare doneness. If the steak is still under temp, return to indirect heat and test again in a couple minutes. If you prefer a rare steak, pull it off the grill when it's 125°F (I don't recommend cooking it past medium-rare; otherwise this lean cut becomes quite dry).

✳ Transfer the steak to a platter or shallow bowl, cover with foil, and let it rest for 10 minutes.

✳ Meanwhile, add the lemon to the grill, cut-side down, and cook until nice and charred, about 5 minutes.

✳ Once the steak has rested, carefully remove the meat from the bone and slice the meat crosswise and against the grain into ½-inch-thick slices. Fan the slices on a serving platter and set aside.

✳ In a small bowl, combine the juices from the platter where the steak was resting with the juice of the grilled lemon and the olive oil. Drizzle the mixture over the sliced steak, season with a pinch of salt—flaky, if you prefer (I use kosher)—and serve.

Dario's Tips for the Perfect Bistecca alla Fiorentina

1. Porterhouse is the preferred cut.

2. Never destroy a steak by cooking it in a cast-iron skillet; the gold standard is a charcoal grill (though gas will do, too).

3. Always let your steak rest in a dish with a drizzle of olive oil and a little salt, then slice it and let the juices marry with the oil.

My only deviation from Dario's advice is on that third point: Dario waits to season until after the steak has been sliced. I prefer salting the meat really well *before* grilling to encourage a nice salty crust to form on the grill, in addition to adding a touch of salt after it's been sliced. Try it both ways and see which you prefer!

NOTES

If your charcoal starts cooling down about halfway through cooking (as it tends to do), add more, as the steak cooks for the second time over indirect heat.

Cooking times will vary depending on the size and type of steak you use. Using an instant-read thermometer is the best way to ensure that it's cooked just right (do NOT cut into your steak to see if it's done; that's how you say good-bye to flavor and juiciness).

This steak makes a gorgeous meal. My favorite accompaniments are Bagna Cauda (page 57) to start, then grilled vegetables (see Verdura a Brace, page 216) and Wine-Roasted Potatoes (page 205). This is the ultimate Italian steak dinner and one of Joe's favorite meals of all time.

Bistecca alla Fiorentina ✳ *page 168*

Seafood Risotto ✳ *page 172*

Seafood RISOTTO

Seafood

2 dozen littleneck clams, soaked in salted water in the refrigerator for 24 hours (see Note, page 111)

2 dozen mussels, debearded and soaked in cold water for 15 minutes (see Note, page 111)

1 tablespoon extra-virgin olive oil

2 garlic cloves, smashed and peeled

Pinch of red pepper flakes

8 ounces shrimp (26/30 count), peeled and deveined

4 ounces squid tubes (bodies) and tentacles, tubes thinly sliced

4 ounces sea scallops, halved or quartered if large

8 ounces cherry tomatoes, halved

When you're sitting in a risotteria by the water in Naples and sipping your spritz, this is what you order. Luckily, my uncle Tony makes the best seafood risotto I've ever had, and he's given me all his tips and tricks to re-create the recipe at home. Now, I know we talked about this being a chapter with dishes for celebrating and having people over, but making this for more than four people will result in hysteria, tears, and gummy rice. (Ask me how I know . . .) Leave this dish for a nice, quiet night with a couple of friends; it's the only thing you need to serve, aside from some crusty bread.

✳ *Prepare the seafood:* Drain the clams and mussels and give them a good scrub. In a medium saucepan over medium heat, add the clams and mussels, cover, and steam until they open, 3 to 4 minutes. Transfer them to a bowl and discard any that haven't opened. Remove the meat from the shells (discard the shells) and transfer any liquid from the bowl into a small bowl or measuring cup.

✳ In a large shallow Dutch oven or large heavy pot, combine the oil, garlic, and pepper flakes and sauté the garlic over medium heat, stirring often, until it begins to lightly brown, about 2 minutes. Add the shrimp, squid, and scallops and toss to coat in the garlic-infused oil. Add the tomatoes and cook until the shrimp have turned pink and the scallops and squid are opaque and firm, about 4 minutes. Transfer the mixture to a shallow bowl and set aside. Do not clean out the pot.

✳ *Make the risotto:* In a small saucepan, combine the stock and 2 cups water and bring to a simmer over medium-low heat. Keep at a low simmer as you make the rice.

✳ In the same pot you used for the seafood, combine the oil and onion and cook over medium heat, stirring occasionally, until the onion softens and becomes translucent, about 5 minutes. Add the rice and cook, stirring constantly, just until it begins to turn opaque, about 2 minutes. Stir in the wine and continue stirring as it reduces by half, about 1 minute.

✳ After the wine absorbs into the rice and you don't see any liquid in the bottom of the pot when you move your spoon through the mixture, it's time to add a ladleful of stock. Continue simmering, stirring occasionally, until the liquid is absorbed, about another 3 minutes. Repeat this process, adding stock a ladleful at a time, until the rice is plump and al dente (soft but with a little bit of bite to it), about 18 minutes total.

✳ Add the reserved liquid from the mussels and clams and cook, stirring, until the liquid has been absorbed, about 2 minutes. Add the clams, mussels, cooked seafood/tomato mixture, and 1 more ladleful of stock. Cook until the rice is really tender, no need to stir, adding more stock if needed, about 4 minutes. Remove from the heat, taste, and season with salt, if needed. Sprinkle with parsley and enjoy the best seafood risotto ever.

Risotto

4 cups seafood stock (see Notes)

2 tablespoons extra-virgin olive oil

1 small yellow onion, minced

1 cup Arborio rice

½ cup dry white wine (pinot grigio for me, always)

Kosher salt (optional)

2 tablespoons chopped fresh Italian parsley

NOTES

I use store-bought seafood stock (Better than Bouillon makes a good one), but you could also use the same amount of clam juice or a 50-50 blend of clam juice and water.

You can "dress up" this recipe with lobster or langoustine. Personally, I don't know very many people worthy of my tracking down langoustine for, but if you do, or you go the extra mile of adding a lobster tail, it is very much worth it.

RISO E POLPETTE

While you know that I don't have any patience for fussy recipes, I do not consider these teeny-tiny polpette (meatballs) to fall in that category. Instead, when I make them with my daughter, it takes me back to being her age and doing the very same thing with Nonna and my cousins, especially my favorite cousin, Alessio. After cooking, we'd take a batch down to the beach along with risotto-esque sauced and Parmed rice and sit in the shade in a parking lot to have lunch. After just a bite, I can close my eyes and be back there, sitting in the plastic chairs at that little table with Nonna, and then walking to the shore hand in hand with her after so we could play in the sand. The meatballs may take a little time to make, but it's an important reminder that it's not always about where we're going, but where we are right at this very moment.

✳ *Make the meatballs:* Tear the bread into ½-inch pieces. If it's too difficult to tear that small, you can pulse it in a food processor. Add the bread bits to a small bowl and cover with the milk, nudging the bread to encourage it to stay submerged. Soak for 10 minutes, then squeeze the bread to drain off as much milk as possible. Discard the milk and place the soaked bread in a large bowl.

✳ Add the beef, Parm, parsley, egg, and garlic to the soaked bread. Add a generous pinch (about 1 teaspoon) of salt and mix thoroughly. Use a 1-teaspoon measuring spoon to form the mixture into tiny meatballs. Set aside on a plate or baking sheet.

✳ *Make the meatball sauce:* In a large Dutch oven or large heavy pot, heat the oil over medium heat until shimmering. Add the meatballs and cook until they brown on one side, about 2 minutes. Reduce the heat to low and add the onion. Cover and let the onions soften on top of the meatballs for 2 minutes. (It's easier to do it this way, since it can be time-consuming to flip all the meatballs.)

Meatballs

3 ounces stale Italian bread (see Notes), about 2 (½-inch-thick) slices

½ cup whole milk

1 pound ground beef (I prefer 85% lean)

½ cup freshly grated Parmigiano-Reggiano cheese

¼ cup loosely packed fresh Italian parsley, finely minced

1 large egg

2 garlic cloves, minced

Kosher salt

Meatball Sauce

2 tablespoons extra-virgin olive oil

1 small yellow onion, minced

¾ cup dry red wine (I like merlot)

4½ cups passata (see Notes)

Kosher salt

7 or 8 fresh basil leaves, torn

Recipe continues

Rice

2 cups Arborio rice

Kosher salt

½ cup of freshly grated Parmigiano-Reggiano cheese

Parmigiano-Reggiano cheese, for serving

Fresh basil, for serving

NOTES

If you don't have day-old bread, you can use ¼ cup bread crumbs and add just enough milk (3 to 4 tablespoons) to moisten them.

A typical 24-ounce jar of passata holds about 3 cups, so you'll need 1½ jars. Or if you buy passata in a 17.6-ounce carton, you'll need 2 of them.

✳ Pour in the wine and allow it to reduce by half, about 3 minutes. Give everything a good stir (don't sweat it if any of the meatballs break apart). Pour in the passata, then swirl 1 cup of water in the empty passata jar and add that as well. Add a good pinch of salt and the basil and stir to combine.

✳ Allow the sauce to come up to a boil, reduce the heat to low, cover, and cook for 2 hours. The sauce is ready when it thickens and the meatballs are super tender. Adjust the seasoning with more salt, if needed.

✳ *Cook the rice:* In a large pot, combine 1½ cups of the finished sauce and 7 cups water. Bring to a boil over medium-high heat, add the rice and a good pinch of salt, and reduce the heat to low. Cook until the rice is al dente, about 18 minutes (it will be creamy like risotto). Stir in the Parm, remove the pot from the heat, and let the rice sit, uncovered, for 10 minutes. (It's meant to be thick and creamy and will continue to thicken as it sits.)

✳ Use a scoop of rice to create a bed in a shallow bowl, then add a ladleful of the sauce and meatballs. Finish with a bit of Parm and some torn basil and serve.

Roasted PORK
with Oranges & Bay Leaves

This dish is inspired by Zia Mimma, who is the "fancy" cook in the family and has always made the most delicious roasts with fruit. Especially for Easter, she would prepare these showstopping braised-for-hours dishes, with plums or apricots or oranges meticulously tucked around the edges. Because we Italians love pork and fruit—what's not to love about the amazing combination of savory and sweet?—I wanted to use those same types of flavors but make the dish a little more my style (i.e., *casual*). Now there's barely 5 minutes of prep time and the cooking does all the magic for you, which is what we're going for. But just in case you're concerned, I made this dish for Nonna the last time she was here, and it has her stamp of approval. Serve with braised beans (see Fagioli a Zuppa over Bread, page 74) and Sautéed Escarole (page 199) and it's very hard to beat.

✳ In a small skillet, toast the peppercorns and fennel seeds over low heat until fragrant, about 2 minutes.

✳ Add the toasted spices to a mortar and pestle or a spice grinder and grind until the mixture is mostly pulverized but still has a few bits of peppercorns here and there. Add the salt to the spice mixture and mix to combine. Rub the mixture all over the pork and set aside.

✳ Preheat the oven to 325°F.

✳ In a large ovenproof skillet or shallow Dutch oven, heat 2 tablespoons of the oil over medium-high heat. When the oil starts to lightly smoke, add the pork (fat-side down if it has a thin, fatty layer) and sear until deeply golden on all sides, 10 to 12 minutes total. Transfer the pork to a plate, drain and discard any fat from the pan, and wipe out any burned spices.

✳ Return the pan to medium heat and add the remaining 1 tablespoon oil, the garlic halves, and the shallots, cut-side down. Cook, occasionally swirling the pan, until the garlic and shallots are lightly browned where they're touching the pan, about 2 minutes.

1 tablespoon black peppercorns

½ teaspoon fennel seeds

1 tablespoon kosher salt

4 pounds boneless pork shoulder

3 tablespoons extra-light olive oil or any neutral oil, such as vegetable or canola

1 head garlic, halved horizontally

8 medium to large shallots, unpeeled and halved

1 orange, quartered (I like navel or will use blood oranges or clementines in the winter), unpeeled

5 fresh bay leaves

6 sprigs fresh thyme

1½ cups freshly squeezed orange juice (from about 4 oranges)

2½ cups low-sodium chicken stock

20 pitted prunes

Fresh Italian parsley, for garnish

Recipe continues

✳ Return the pork to the pan, nestling it right in the center. Surround the pork with the orange wedges, bay leaves, and thyme. Pour in the orange juice and chicken stock. Cover the pan or tightly cover with foil, then pop it into the oven to cook for 2 hours.

✳ After 2 hours, increase the temperature to 350°F. Add the prunes, nestling them into the broth. Cook until the pan juices thicken and the pork falls apart when poked with a fork, about 1 more hour.

✳ Allow the roast to rest for 20 minutes before cutting into ½-inch-thick slices (see Note). Arrange the slices on a platter surrounded by the roasted shallots, garlic, prunes, and oranges. Spoon some of the pan juices over the pork to keep it moist, garnish with parsley, and pass the remaining pan juices on the side.

Ham & Fontina
LASAGNA

Béchamel

4 tablespoons unsalted butter

¼ cup all-purpose flour

4 cups whole milk

1 tablespoon Dijon mustard

½ cup freshly grated Parmigiano-Reggiano cheese

Pinch of freshly grated nutmeg (about ¼ teaspoon)

Kosher salt and freshly ground pepper

Ham Filling

2 tablespoons extra-virgin olive oil

1 tablespoon unsalted butter

2 large (but not massive) leeks, trimmed, halved lengthwise, rinsed, and thinly sliced into half-moons (see Note)

4 garlic cloves, minced

5 sprigs of fresh thyme, leaves stripped from the stem

3 cups chopped ham (deli roasted ham is fine)

1 cup fresh whole-milk ricotta cheese

NOTE

I use leeks instead of onions here, but you be the boss of your kitchen and use what you like because last I checked, Italy has no leeks.

In my first book, I included a recipe for bow tie pasta with cream and ham because it was a weekly staple that my mom made for us as kids, and needless to say, it was a huge hit. But I think we can agree that we can all use even *more* pasta, cream, and ham in our lives, so I got the blessing from my mama to turn this signature dish into a lasagna. It elevates the original just a touch and makes it special enough for company or even a holiday. It would be right at home on Christmas Day if, like me, you always do a stuffed pasta with the rest of the spread. If you roast a turkey *and* a ham on Thanksgiving like we do, simply freeze the leftover ham, so you have enough to make the lasagna for Christmas. I've started this tradition, and now my sister says she would "un-sister" me if I ever make a regular lasagna instead of this one!

✳ *Start by making the béchamel:* Melt the butter in a large saucepan over medium heat. Whisk in the flour and continue whisking for about 1 minute, just to cook off some of the raw flavor from the flour. Whisk in the milk and continue whisking until the sauce thickens, about 3 minutes, being sure to get into the corners of the pan so nothing burns. Remove the pan from the heat. Stir in the Dijon, Parm, and nutmeg, then season to taste with salt and pepper. Set aside.

✳ *Make the filling:* In a large skillet over medium heat, add the olive oil and butter. When the butter is melted and begins to foam, add the leeks. Season with salt and pepper and sauté until softened, stirring occasionally, about 10 minutes. Add the garlic and thyme leaves and cook just until they release their fragrance, about 1 more minute. Remove the pan from the heat and stir in the ham and ricotta. Set aside to cool slightly.

✳ *Assemble:* Preheat the oven to 375°F. Use the butter to lightly grease a 9x13-inch casserole dish. Set ¼ of the mozzarella, ¼ of the Parm, and ¼ of the pecorino aside.

✻ Add ¾ cup of the sauce to the bottom of the casserole dish, followed by a quarter of the lasagna noodles. Spread ⅓ of the filling over the top, followed by a quarter of the fontina and the remaining (not counting the reserved cheeses for the topping) mozzarella, Parm, and pecorino. Continue this process until your top layer is the last of the noodles, followed by the last of the sauce.

✻ Cover the pan with aluminum foil and bake for 45 minutes. Remove the foil, add the reserved mozzarella, Parm, and pecorino, and bake for another 30 minutes, or until the top is golden brown and bubbly. Allow the lasagna to cool for a minimum of 45 minutes before slicing and serving.

Assembly

Unsalted butter, at room temperature, for greasing

8 ounces fresh mozzarella cheese, thinly sliced

½ cup freshly grated Parmigiano-Reggiano cheese

½ cup freshly grated pecorino cheese

1 pound no-cook lasagna noodles

5 ounces fontina cheese, grated

TORTELLINI
in Brodo di Verdura

Brodo di Verdura

1 pound peeled and cubed butternut squash (from 1 small squash)

2 medium russet potatoes

1 medium yellow onion, chopped

2 medium carrots, peeled and chopped

2 small zucchini, diced

2 celery stalks, diced

8 ounces green beans, trimmed and roughly chopped

½ cup passata, or 2 plum tomatoes or tomatoes on the vine, chopped

5 or 6 fresh basil leaves

2 tablespoons extra-virgin olive oil

Kosher salt

To Finish

Kosher salt

12 ounces dried three-cheese tortellini (I like Barilla; see Notes)

Extra-virgin olive oil, for drizzling

Freshly grated Parmigiano-Reggiano cheese, for serving

My daughter, Mia, is not always the most, shall we say, *obliging* dinner guest, but if there is one thing I know she will always gladly tuck into, it's a bowl of this rich, silky soup studded with cheese-stuffed tortellini or ditalini. It never gets old making it for her, either, because I know that she's getting in all her vegetables, and also because this is what Nonna made for all of us when we were just beginning to eat solids. That said, it's not just meant to be served to children. It's a comfort to anyone, and there's not much that's better than a bowlful with an extra sprinkle of Parm on a blistering-cold January day. It's also a great way to sneak veg into a meal for picky little ones—or adults.

✳ *Make the brodo di verdura:* In a large soup pot, combine the squash, potatoes, onion, carrots, zucchini, celery, green beans, passata (or tomatoes), basil, and oil. Add 16 cups water and bring to a boil over medium-high heat. Add a generous pinch of salt, reduce the heat to low, partially cover, and cook for 2 hours. You want the vegetables to be cooked down and falling apart, aka "ugly tender."

✳ Use a slotted spoon or spider to transfer the veggies to a food mill (see Notes) and process the vegetables over a bowl. Return the puree to the pot of broth and bring to a low boil over medium-low heat. Reduce to a simmer and keep the soup at a simmer until ready to serve.

✳ *To finish:* Fill a medium pot with water, bring to a boil over medium-high heat, and add a moderate pinch of salt—just enough to make the water taste slightly salty. Add the tortellini and cook for 2 minutes less than the package directions.

✳ Drain the tortellini and add to the soup. Cook for 2 more minutes to let the flavors meld. Adjust the seasoning with more salt, if needed.

✳ Serve with an extra drizzle of olive oil and a spoonful of Parm.

NOTES

You can't go wrong with any small shape of pasta such as ditalini, acini di pepe, or stelline. Use about 8 ounces and cook it right into the soup; it'll thicken up quite a bit, but that's part of the charm.

And don't turn your nose up at dried box tortellini! For the ease of always being able to find them at my grocery store and having them on hand, as well as the confidence that they'll always deliver flavor-wise, I'd pick them over fresh any day.

Last, you can use a blender or food processor to puree the soup. Nonna liked a food mill because she could discard the vegetable skins, which she said would "upset a baby's stomach."

Fresh PASTA
with Pesto Genovese

I had to give you this recipe for a couple reasons. For one, I don't think an Italian cookbook could really call itself that if it didn't include fresh pasta. Secondly, it's the best opportunity to give you my godmother Zia Mimma's pesto recipe. She was the first person to make it for me, and I remember it so vividly. When she was in her twenties and wanting to make a little cash, she worked as a salesperson for the Bimbo all-in-one food processor and would do demos for how to make things—one of which was pesto. At the time—this was the mid-nineties—pesto was a new thing in southern Italy. People were like, "We don't do this in Naples; we like red sauce." But for me, it was love at first bite. And sure enough, after doing enough of these demos at people's houses and offering them a spoonful of this vibrantly fresh, fragrant sauce, they fell in love, too. So for me, fresh pasta and pesto go hand in hand, especially since the Bimbo (see Note) could do both! Now I make pesto all summer long and either store it in the fridge for up to a week or in the freezer to enjoy through the fall and winter months—with pasta or in sauces, soups, stews, you name it!

✳ *Make the pasta:* Add the 00 flour to a large cutting board and, using your fingers, make a well in the middle. Add the eggs, oil, and salt to the well, then use a fork to begin whisking the eggs, gradually incorporating flour from the sides of the well. Eventually the mixture will feel very dry and crumbly, which is when you can use your hands to start bringing the mixture together and kneading. (A dough scraper works well here for gathering up the flour easily.)

✳ Knead for a good 10 minutes until the mixture forms a dough. Alternatively, you could pulse the mixture in a food processor until the dough is nice and smooth. I promise that the dry and crumbly texture will get there, but if it's not looking promising, you can add a tablespoon or two of water—you won't need more than that. Form the dough into a ball and wrap it in plastic wrap. Allow the dough to rest at room temperature for 45 minutes.

Pasta

3 cups 00 flour, plus more for dusting

5 large eggs

1 tablespoon extra-virgin olive oil

¾ teaspoon kosher salt, plus a pinch

Semolina flour, for dusting

Pesto

4 cups packed fresh basil leaves

¼ cup pine nuts, toasted until fragrant in a dry pan

2 garlic cloves, peeled and smashed

2 teaspoons finely grated lemon zest (about ½ lemon)

2 teaspoons fresh lemon juice

Kosher salt

½ cup extra-virgin olive oil

½ cup freshly grated Parmigiano-Reggiano, plus more for serving

Recipe continues

You don't need a Bimbo, or a food processor, to make pesto. You can do what Nonna Laura really did, which was make it by hand with a mortar and pestle. And if you want the fresh pasta experience but don't want to make it, you can always buy it from an Italian market. Or you could cook dried pasta (see my favorites on page 18), toss it with the pesto, and call it dinner.

To store the pesto in the refrigerator, add it to a jar with a tight-fitting lid and drizzle a thin layer of olive oil over the top, which will keep it from oxidizing. Store for up to 1 week. To freeze, spoon the pesto into the wells of an ice cube tray, drizzle with a thin layer of olive oil, and freeze. Transfer the frozen cubes to a freezer-safe zip-top bag and store for up to 6 months.

❋ *Meanwhile, make the pesto:* In a food processor, add the basil, pine nuts, garlic, lemon zest, and lemon juice with a pinch of salt. Pulse until the mixture is finely chopped. With the motor running, stream in the olive oil, pausing halfway through to use a spatula to scrape down the sides of the bowl. Add the cheese, pulse a couple times to mix, then transfer the pesto to a container with a tight-fitting lid. For storage information, see Notes.

❋ Now it's time to roll out the pasta. Get a pasta machine ready, line a baking sheet with a lint-free kitchen towel, and sprinkle some semolina on top. Keep the semolina nearby, along with a bit of 00 flour.

❋ Fill a large pot with water, add a generous pinch of salt, and bring to a boil over medium-high heat.

❋ Cut the dough into 6 equal pieces. Set 1 piece aside and cover the rest with a lint-free kitchen towel. Use your hands to shape the dough into a rectangle, then flatten it to fit into the pasta machine. Beginning with the widest setting, pass the dough through the pasta machine. Repeat twice more to ensure that there are no air bubbles in the dough. Decrease the width setting to the next smallest and pass the dough through again. Continue doing this until you've reached the thinnest setting.

❋ Cut the sheet of pasta into your desired shape (I use my machine to make fettuccine), then sprinkle some of the semolina over the noodles and toss to coat well, which will keep them from sticking together. Twirl them into a little "nest" on the baking sheet, uncovered, while you continue rolling and cutting the remaining dough.

❋ Working in batches (I boil the pasta in three parts), cook the pasta in the salted boiling water until al dente, about 3 minutes. Using tongs, carefully transfer the pasta to a bowl and repeat with the remaining pasta. When finished, reserve about ½ cup of the starchy cooking water.

❋ Toss the pasta with the pesto (I use all of it), half of the cooking water (you want just enough to help the pesto cling to the pasta), and more grated Parm until well coated. Serve immediately, as the pesto will brown as it sits.

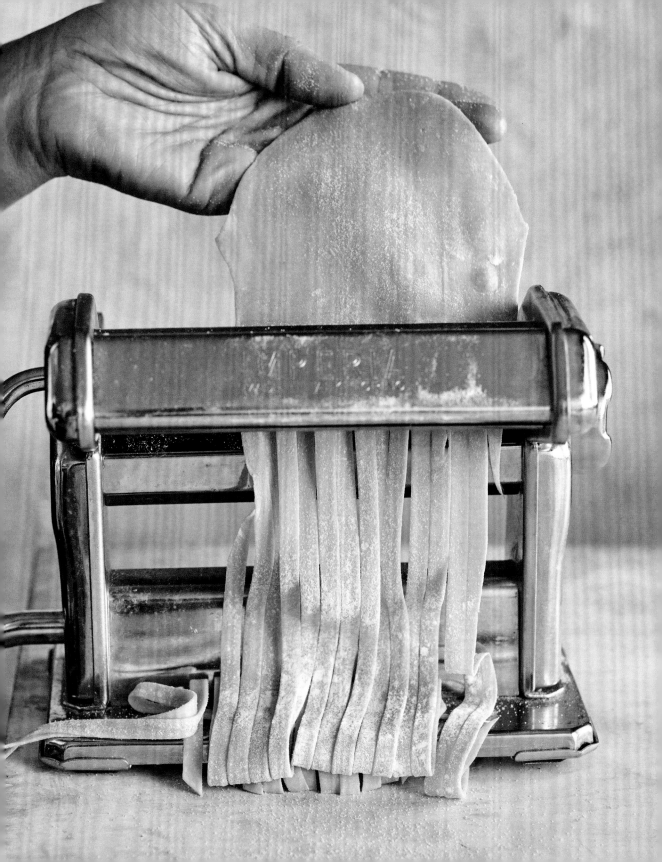

The Main Event: NONNA'S SUNDAY SAUCE

Meatball mixture (from Riso e Polpette, page 175)

¼ cup extra-virgin olive oil

1½ pounds country-style pork ribs (4 or 5 ribs)

1½ pounds boneless beef chuck roast, cut into 3-inch pieces

Kosher salt

1 large yellow onion, diced

1 cup dry red wine (I use merlot)

3 (24-ounce) bottles passata or 3 (28-ounce) cans tomato puree

Large handful of fresh basil leaves (about ½ cup)

Cooked medium tube pasta, such as paccheri or rigatoni, for serving

This is it. The sugo, the sauce, heaven in a pot, liquid gold—whatever you want to call it, this is what was simmering on my nonna's stove from the time she got up Sunday morning until midday when we sat down to lunch. The browned bits of Italian sausage and beef, and sometimes Bracioletti in Sugo (page 130), slowly softened and submitted into the tomatoey bath perfumed with red wine (merlot, always), aromatics, and basil. The most important element—besides love, obviously—is time. The more the sauce bubbles away, the more it concentrates in flavor until it's ready to be spooned over cavatelli, spaghetti, or a heel of crusty bread. Every household has their own recipe for making their Sunday sauce, and this one's been in our family for generations. Whenever I make it, I like to picture all the nonnas in their kitchens, surrounded by all the people they care about the most, and remember that as long as this sauce is on my stove, I'm never alone.

❋ Make the meatball mixture as directed and then form into meatballs the size of golf balls (you should get about 20). In a large Dutch oven or large heavy pot, heat the oil over medium-high heat until shimmering. Add the meatballs and cook until seared and golden brown all over, about 5 minutes total. Transfer the meatballs to a platter and set aside; do not wipe out the pan.

❋ Season the ribs and chuck roast with salt. Return the pot you used to sear the meatballs to medium-high heat and, working in batches, add the ribs and chuck roast pieces in a single layer. Cook until golden brown all over, about 5 minutes total. Transfer the meat to the plate with the meatballs and set aside. (Don't be afraid to really stack 'em up! The meatballs can handle it.)

* Add the onion to the pan you used to sear the meat and sauté until tender, stirring occasionally, 3 to 5 minutes. Return the ribs and chuck to the pan and add the wine. Allow the wine to reduce by half, about 2 minutes, then add the passata. Add about ⅓ cup of water to each bottle, cover and give it a shake, and add that to the pot as well. Sprinkle in a good pinch of salt and nestle the meatballs in the sauce along with the basil. Bring the sauce to a boil, then reduce the heat to low. Partially cover the pot and simmer for 3 hours, or until the chuck is fall-apart tender and the meat from the ribs easily falls away from the bone.

* Adjust the seasoning to taste and serve with pasta. Store leftovers in an airtight container for up to 3 days in the fridge or up to 3 months in the freezer (see Note).

NOTE

Since this sauce freezes so nicely, I like to make a double batch so I can have sugo on a weekday whenever I'm in the mood.

Seriously Good
Vegetable
SIDES &
SALADS

✳ (That I *Often*
Eat as DINNER
with Some
CRUSTY Bread) ✳

I WILL DIE ON THE HILL *that this chapter* is my favorite in the book. Those are big words. But anyone who knows me knows that I absolutely love vegetables—as Italians generally do. We tend to grow a lot of our own, so there's always an abundance of them, and we're not of the opinion that you need to treat them like they're your stepcousin that you see only once a year and don't particularly like—vegetables should be celebrated and not just tolerated.

In addition to being delicious in their own right, vegetables have a way of making everything *else* on the table taste that much better because they bring balance, freshness, and texture to a meal. Say you're having a rich steak for dinner, you need something bright, bitter, or crunchy alongside to take that richness down a couple notches. That's where my vegetables come in. These recipes mix and match seamlessly with any of the mains in the book and are the easiest way to make a meal that much more substantial and special— which is basically how I'd build a dinner on a Saturday or Sunday. Or, if you feel inspired to make an entire meal out of these dishes and nothing else, that would absolutely be correct, too.

What I also love about these recipes is that they're going to get you all the way through the year because most of them are great even with grocery store produce that's not necessarily in season. That said, you will always get the most flavor and the most bang for your buck if you're cooking with what's growing at that moment. ✳

Broccoli Rabe

2 bunches of broccoli rabe

⅓ cup olive oil

5 garlic cloves, smashed and peeled

½ teaspoon dried red pepper flakes, or to taste

Kosher salt

Crusty Italian bread, for serving (optional)

The joke in my family is that when I was two or three, I choked on broccoli rabe because I was grabbing it by the handful and shoving it into my mouth. What can I say? Broccoli rabe was, and always will be, my all-time favorite vegetable. If you like a mild veg, then maybe spinach is more your speed, but if you're into a punchy, delicious green that can really hold its own against fish or a steak, then you go with broccoli rabe. There is this crazy idea out there that you need to blanch your broccoli rabe before sautéing it in order to cook out the bitterness, but to my Italian heart, that's nonsense! That bitterness is what makes it so special. I cook three or four bunches at a time at least a couple days a week and serve it with sausage or pork chops, or my husband has it with cutlets and sharp provolone stacked on a sandwich. We eat it hot, at room temp, or cold straight out of the fridge.

✳ Before even untying the bunches of broccoli rabe, trim about 3 inches from the bottom of the stems. Go ahead and separate your stems, and if you have any thick, woody-looking ones, strip off the leaves and florets to use and discard the thick stems. The other stems can be chopped and added to a large bowl along with the leaves and florets. Cover with cold water, rinse thoroughly, drain, and set aside.

✳ In a large skillet (I use my 12-inch for this) set over medium heat, combine the oil, garlic, and red pepper flakes, occasionally swirling the pan, until the garlic begins to lightly brown around the edges, about 2 minutes. Add the broccoli rabe followed by 1 cup of water. Cover and cook for 5 minutes. Remove the lid and give the broccoli rabe a good toss, since at this point they will have wilted a bit and will be easier to maneuver. Sprinkle with salt.

✳ Add another 1 cup water, cover, and cook for 10 more minutes. Remove the lid and cook for 5 minutes so the water can evaporate. The broccoli rabe should be nice and tender and deeply green but not mushy. Serve with bread, if desired. (And let's be honest, it's desired.)

Arugula
with Fennel & Balsamic

One of my favorite things to do with my nonna was to pick wild arugula down by the shore. It was at a time when this hot, peppery leafy green was still a novelty; you couldn't just go to the store and buy it. Then, when we got home, my grandma would make a salad just like this one. The arugula would be so intensely flavored that to help tame its heat, she'd add cool, sweet fennel sliced very thinly, almost like a carpaccio. Then she'd toss it with lots of olive oil and balsamic and call it a day. Because I love the way these flavors complement just about any dish, and since I'm of the opinion that a salad does not have to be complicated, I frequently have this on my table along with whatever else I'm serving. Sometimes I even enjoy it on its own for lunch, or with some good canned tuna or leftover roasted or grilled chicken.

✳ In a large bowl, combine the arugula, fennel, and shallot. Drizzle with the olive oil, balsamic vinegar, and red wine vinegar, add a pinch of salt, and lightly toss to coat. Enjoy right away!

5 ounces baby arugula

1 small fennel bulb, trimmed, halved, cored, and very thinly sliced (I like a mandoline for this)

1 medium shallot, halved and thinly sliced

2 tablespoons extra-virgin olive oil

1 tablespoon balsamic vinegar

2 teaspoons red wine vinegar

Kosher salt

SPINACI
al Limone

1 pound baby spinach

2 garlic cloves, smashed
and peeled

1 tablespoon extra-virgin
olive oil

Kosher salt

Juice of ½ lemon,
or to taste

When I say I'm making a side of spinach, this is what I'm talking about. It takes about five minutes; and it doesn't call for more than garlic, olive oil, and lemon juice because you want to accentuate the delicate flavor of the greens, not cover them up. It's the only way spinach was ever prepared in my nonna's kitchen, and it is most certainly good enough for me.

✳ In a large pot, bring ½ cup water to a boil over medium-low heat. Add the spinach, and cook undisturbed, covered, for 5 minutes, until cooked down almost completely.

✳ Give the spinach a good toss, then transfer it to a shallow bowl. Tuck the garlic cloves in the hot spinach, drizzle with the oil, and sprinkle with a good amount of salt. When ready to serve, squeeze lemon over the spinach and enjoy.

Sautéed ESCAROLE
with Olives & Pine Nuts
(& Escarole Pie)

My nonno's best friend Vittorio was a farmer, and at the end of the week, they'd barter—Nonno's fish for Vittorio's vegetables. Sometimes Nonno would come home with a crateful of escarole, which is a bitter green that's part of the chicory family (think endive and radicchio). And when he did, Nonna would make us this dish. To this day, it is my favorite way to cook and eat escarole, sautéed until buttery tender then tossed with toasted pine nuts and briny olives. Also, I, like Nonna, double this recipe so I can make Escarole Pie (page 201), one of the most delicious things on the planet that is usually served alongside Pizza Ripiena (page 147) for Easter or Christmas Eve lunch, or is the ultimate make-once-eat-all-week dish.

✢ Fill a large pot with water, and add a generous pinch of salt, and bring to a boil over high heat. Add the escarole, and when the water returns to a boil, cook for 5 minutes, until the escarole just wilts and starts to get tender. Drain (see Notes) and immediately rinse with cold water to stop the escarole from cooking further. Once the escarole has cooled, squeeze out any excess water and set aside.

✢ In a large skillet over medium heat, add the olive oil, pine nuts, garlic, and red pepper flakes. Cook, stirring occasionally, until the garlic is sizzling and the pine nuts are golden, about 2 minutes, then stir in the escarole and olives. Cook for 10 minutes, until the escarole is nice and tender. Taste and if needed, season the escarole with more salt and a bit of pepper before serving with escarole pie.

Kosher salt and freshly ground pepper

3 bunches of escarole, core trimmed and outer leaves removed and halved horizontally

3 tablespoons extra-virgin olive oil

¼ cup pine nuts

3 garlic cloves, thinly sliced

Heavy pinch of dried red pepper flakes

½ cup pitted Kalamata or Gaeta olives, halved

Escarole Pie (recipe follows), for serving

NOTES

I grew up eating this dish with anchovies, but I took them out because I know they can be divisive. But if you're feeling a little adventurous and want to make this dish even tastier, add a few anchovy fillets when sautéing your garlic and allow them to melt into the oil.

Don't throw away your escarole cooking water! You can use it as vegetable stock or to cook rice, or you could add some chopped vegetables and a bouillon cube and have yourself some delicious, nutrient-rich broth.

Recipe continues

Escarole Pie

MAKES 1 LARGE PIZZA
(easily serves 10+)

Dough for Pizza Ripiena
(page 147)

Sautéed Escarole
(page 199)

✳ Prep the dough just as you would for Pizza Ripiena. While the dough rises, make your escarole and set it aside to cool completely.

✳ Preheat the oven to 400°F.

✳ Follow the steps for assembling Pizza Ripiena, using the cooled escarole as the filling. Bake for 30 to 40 minutes, until deeply browned.

✳ Allow the pie to cool for 20 minutes before inverting onto a wire rack. Let the pie cool completely, about 30 more minutes, before slicing and serving.

✳ Store leftovers in a sealed container in the refrigerator for up to 4 days. Enjoy cold as a snack or a meal.

PEPERONATA

¼ cup extra-virgin
olive oil

4 medium bell peppers
(about 1½ pounds,
any color but green),
stemmed, seeded, and cut
into large chunks

1 medium yellow onion,
cut into large chunks

1 small fennel bulb,
trimmed, halved, cored,
and cut about the same
size as the peppers

4 garlic cloves, minced

½ pound (3 to 4) tomatoes
on the vine, cut into big
chunks

1 tablespoon whole fresh
rosemary needles

5 or 6 fresh basil leaves,
torn

Kosher salt and freshly
ground black pepper

Handful of pitted
Castelvetrano olives
(scant ⅓ cup)

1 tablespoon red wine
vinegar

¼ cup loosely packed fresh
Italian parsley leaves,
finely chopped

This pepper stew doesn't come from my family recipe box, but it definitely feels like it could have. I grew up growing and eating a ton of bell peppers, but they were mostly fried and served alongside pork chops (see page 87). Now that I have a garden of my own, I still grow a lot of peppers; in fact, my husband decides every year that we need to grow about 100 different varieties (okay, maybe just 10 or 11, and to me they still all taste the same). And at the height of pepper season, I love making peperonata, a Southern Italian dish that calls for cooking down the peppers until they're soft and almost jammy with tomatoes, lots of garlic, and olives. It's fantastic served alongside grilled meats or fish, or cold on a piece of toast with sharp cheese. Or you could even leave out the olives and puree it with a little stock to make a creamy pepper soup. Tomato bisque who? We don't know her; we've got pepper bisque.

✳ Heat the oil in a large heavy pot over medium heat. Once it shimmers, add the peppers, onion, and fennel. Cook, stirring often, until the vegetables cook down and develop some color, about 20 minutes. If after 15 minutes they aren't browning, increase the heat to medium-high. Once the vegetables develop color, add the garlic. (If you increased the heat to finish browning, reduce it to medium before adding the garlic.) Cook until the garlic perfumes the vegetables, about 1 more minute.

✳ Stir in the tomatoes, rosemary, and basil and season with salt and pepper. Partially cover and cook, stirring occasionally, for 20 minutes. Everything should be cooked down and almost jammy. During the last few minutes of cooking, stir in the whole olives and vinegar.

✳ Remove the pot from the heat, stir in the parsley, and serve hot or at room temperature.

Wine-Roasted POTATOES

The only thing I really need to say here is that these are the best potatoes in the whole wide world. They are very much inspired by the potatoes we used to pick up on weekends at the polleria that had been roasted beneath racks of white-wine-misted rotisserie chickens and bathed in all those drippings (more on that on page 159). So while it might seem odd that these get cooked in liquid—chicken broth and white wine—you've got to trust the magic of a spud in a hot oven (not to mention the roasted garlic and rosemary combo)! They get lusciously tender and fluffy, soaking up all of that flavor in the cooking liquid. This is really the only potato recipe you need.

✻ Preheat the oven to 425°F.

✻ Fill a large saucepan with water and bring to a boil over medium-high heat. Add the potatoes with a generous pinch of salt and boil for 10 minutes, just to partially cook the potatoes. Drain and let the potatoes sit in the colander for 5 minutes.

✻ In a small bowl or measuring cup, whisk together the stock, wine, and olive oil with a pinch of salt and pepper. Set aside.

✻ Lightly oil a 9 x 13-inch baking pan (metal and nonstick, if you have it). Add the potatoes cut-side down and pour the wine mixture over the top. Nestle the garlic cloves among the potatoes, sprinkle with the rosemary, and roast undisturbed for 45 minutes. The potatoes are done when tender and lightly golden with a deeply golden-brown bottom. Remove from the oven and serve; no need to discard the garlic—it gets divinely roasty, crispy, and sweet.

2 pounds russet potatoes, peeled, halved, and cut lengthwise into 6 to 8 wedges

Kosher salt and freshly ground black pepper

¾ cup low-sodium chicken stock

½ cup dry white wine (pinot grigio for me, always)

¼ cup extra-virgin olive oil, plus more for greasing

8 garlic cloves, smashed but unpeeled

1 long sprig of fresh rosemary (about 4 inches), needles removed

Roasted CAULIFLOWER
with Green Olives

1 medium head of cauliflower, outer leaves trimmed and stem trimmed so the head sits flat and upright (see Note)

3 tablespoons extra-virgin olive oil

2 tablespoons freshly grated Parmigiano-Reggiano cheese

2 garlic cloves, grated or minced

Kosher salt and freshly ground black pepper

Handful of Castelvetrano olives (pitted or not, up to you!)

2 tablespoons (more or less) chopped fresh Italian parsley

Juice of ½ lemon

NOTE

You might be wondering why I don't just have you start with cauliflower florets from the beginning instead of parboiling the whole head. It's because I find that they absorb too much liquid and you never end up with perfectly roasted cauliflower.

Roasting cauliflower is the best way to serve it when you want to intensify and celebrate its natural flavor. Plenty of savory Parm and garlic plus briny olives and bright lemon juice balance the whole thing out and bring the dish to life. It's great as a side or cold in a salad the next day. (And, by the way, this won't stink up the house because you're throwing the cauliflower in a hot oven and letting it do the work for you.)

✳ Fill a large pot (I use my Dutch oven; the cauliflower needs to easily fit within the pot) with about an inch of water. Add the cauliflower, stem-side down, and cover. Bring to a boil over medium-high heat, then reduce to a simmer over medium. Simmer for 15 minutes, until the cauliflower is cooked about halfway, then remove it to a cutting board (I use a kitchen spider for this) and allow it to cool slightly.

✳ Preheat the oven to 425°F. Line a baking sheet with parchment paper and set aside.

✳ In a small bowl, stir together the oil, Parmesan, and garlic. Set aside.

✳ Cut the cauliflower into large bite-size pieces and add them to a large bowl. Season with plenty of salt and pepper, then drizzle over the Parmesan mixture. Toss to coat well. (It's okay if a few bits break apart.) Add the olives and give one more toss.

✳ Spread the cauliflower and olives over the prepared sheet pan. Bake for 20 minutes, or until the cauliflower is deeply golden brown around the edges. Transfer to a platter, sprinkle over the parsley and a squeeze of lemon, and serve.

Melanzane
a Funghetti

2 pounds medium-firm eggplants (preferably small Italian ones; see Note), diced into 1-inch cubes

1 tablespoon kosher salt, plus more to taste

½ cup extra-light olive oil, plus more as needed

2 garlic cloves, smashed and peeled

¾ pound tomatoes on the vine, diced

5 or 6 fresh basil leaves, torn, plus more for garnish

After marinated eggplant, this is the second most popular way to eat eggplant in my family. It literally translates to "mushroom-style eggplant"—there are no mushrooms involved, but it describes how you can take a vegetable with a lot of moisture and cook it down without it turning to mush. The secret is pressing the eggplant with salt, which is essential for giving the eggplant great texture and helping it absorb all that beautiful garlic flavor. So don't be tempted to skip it! You could serve this on its own; or you could add some pasta and a little Parm or pecorino plus a splash of the pasta cooking water for a phenomenal vegetarian main; or you could take the heel of a loaf of bread, scoop out the center, add the eggplant to the hollowed center, top with a piece of mozzarella, and call it lunch.

✳ In a colander, toss the eggplant with the salt to coat. Cover the eggplant with a plate small enough to fit within the colander even when weighed down. Set something heavy on top (I use a few cans of tomatoes) and let the eggplant compress and drain for 1 hour at room temperature. Meanwhile, line a platter or baking sheet with paper towels and set aside.

✳ Quickly rinse the eggplant—emphasis on *quickly* because it will otherwise absorb too much water; you just want to rinse off the salt. Take a handful of the eggplant and squeeze to get rid of any excess water, then transfer it to the prepared platter or baking sheet. Add another paper towel on top and press the eggplant to absorb as much water as you can. Repeat with the remaining eggplant.

✳ Line a plate with paper towels and set aside. In a large skillet (I use a 12-inch), heat the oil over medium heat. Once it's shimmering, add about a quarter of the eggplant. Cook, stirring often, until the eggplant develops a deep golden color on all sides, 3 to 4 minutes. Use a spatula or tongs to transfer the eggplant to the paper-towel-lined plate and repeat with the remaining eggplant, adding more oil if needed.

＊ Remove all but two tablespoons of oil from the pan. Over medium heat, add the garlic and sauté, stirring often, until it begins to lightly brown at the edges, about 2 minutes. Add the tomatoes, a pinch of salt, and the basil and cook for about 5 minutes, until the tomatoes begin to break down and thicken. Remove the pan from the heat, adjust the seasoning with more salt if necessary, and serve with extra basil on top.

NOTE

If using standard large eggplant, you might want to buy an extra one because you will need to trim a lot of the soft, spongy center that's full of seeds. Otherwise, it will turn to mush.

Classic
PANZANELLA

During my visit to Tuscany, I stayed in a gorgeous villa on top of a mountain where we had a house chef (I was really roughing it, I know). One night he made us an authentic Tuscan panzanella, which was nothing more than tomatoes, a little onion, some oil, oregano, and vinegar tossed together with stale bread—and it was the best version of the dish I'd ever had. What he told me was to not think of it as tomato salad with bread, but rather bread salad with tomatoes. The trick is to not take away any of the flavor from what was once really good bread soaking up all those sweet, delicious juices. I've never made it any other way since.

✳ In a large bowl, combine the tomatoes, onion, oil, red wine vinegar, balsamic vinegar, garlic, oregano, and a pinch of salt. Allow the mixture to sit for 10 minutes.

✳ Add the bread and torn basil to the tomato mixture and toss everything for 1 to 2 minutes to ensure that the bread begins to soak up the dressing. Cover the bowl with plastic wrap and allow the salad to sit at room temperature for 15 minutes before serving.

✳ When the salad is ready, transfer it to a shallow bowl or platter. If you want to be fancy, serve with a side of fresh mozzarella and Kalamata or Gaeta olives.

1½ pounds tomatoes on the vine, cut into large chunks

¼ small red onion, thinly sliced

¼ cup extra-virgin olive oil

1 tablespoon red wine vinegar

2 teaspoons balsamic vinegar

1 garlic clove, grated

1 teaspoon dried Italian oregano

Kosher salt

½ pound day-old Italian bread (not rock-hard), preferably ciabatta, cut into 1-inch pieces

7 or 8 fresh basil leaves, torn

Fresh mozzarella, for serving (optional)

Kalamata or Gaeta olives, for serving (optional)

Baked "Unstuffed" TOMATOES

2 pounds tomatoes on the vine, cut into thick wedges

5 tablespoons extra-virgin olive oil

Kosher salt

8 ounces stale Italian bread such as ciabatta or baguette

¼ cup loosely packed fresh Italian parsley

2 garlic cloves, peeled

5 or 6 fresh basil leaves

⅓ cup freshly grated Parmigiano-Reggiano cheese

My nonna stuffed her tomatoes. I do not. I love the flavor of them, but I hate making them, so I came up with my own version that has all the same ingredients as the original but takes a fraction of the time. Because these are way too good to be made only on those rare occasions when you have extra time to spend in the kitchen. These may not look as cute as Nonna's, but we don't go for cute; we go for good and easy. It's also a recipe that's particularly great for off-season tomatoes.

✳ Preheat the oven to 400°F.

✳ In a small casserole dish just big enough to hold the tomatoes snugly in a single layer, drizzle 2 tablespoons of the oil over the tomatoes and season with salt. Bake for 10 minutes while you make the topping.

✳ To make the topping, combine the bread, parsley, garlic, and basil in a food processor. Pulse until finely chopped. Add the Parm and the remaining 3 tablespoons of olive oil and pulse until everything is well combined.

✳ Scatter the topping over the partially baked tomatoes and return to the oven to bake until golden brown and crispy, 20 to 25 minutes. Allow to cool slightly before serving.

Italian CHOPPED *Salad*

This is one of my favorite salads, namely because it has all my favorite things from the traditional antipasti spreads that I grew up eating—notably lots of salumi and sharp cheese, plus a pungent, anchovy-laced Caesar-ish dressing to bring it all together. It's like an Italian sub or hoagie (or whatever you like to call it) in salad form. I double or even triple the dressing and keep it in the fridge for any last-minute weekday salads, tossing with orzo, or drizzling over grilled vegetables (see Verdura a Brace, page 216). With fresh buffalo mozzarella on top? Ugh; get outta town.

✳ *Make the dressing:* In a jar with a tight-fitting lid, add the oil, vinegar, Parm, garlic, Dijon, anchovy paste, and oregano. Season with a pinch of salt and pepper and shake to incorporate well.

✳ *Make the salad:* In a large salad bowl, add the tomatoes and season them with a pinch of salt. Add the romaine, radicchio, salami, provolone, peperoncini, and onion and drizzle with about half of the dressing (use more or less, depending on your preference). Store the remainder of the dressing in the fridge. Give everything a good toss to combine, then serve right away.

NOTE

If making this salad ahead of time, store the dressing in the jar (which can last in the fridge for up to 1 week) and wait to toss everything else together until you're ready to serve.

Dressing

¼ cup extra-virgin olive oil

3 tablespoons red wine vinegar

2 tablespoons freshly grated Parmigiano-Reggiano cheese

2 garlic cloves, minced

2 teaspoons Dijon mustard

1 teaspoon anchovy paste

1 teaspoon dried Italian oregano

Kosher salt and freshly ground black pepper

Salad

1 pint cherry tomatoes, quartered

Kosher salt

1 large head of romaine, shredded

1 medium head of radicchio, shredded

6 ounces salami (I like soppressata), cut into ¼-inch-thick strips

6 ounces provolone, cut into ¼-inch-thick strips

¼ cup peperoncini rings

½ small red onion, halved and thinly sliced

Vegetables

2 pounds assorted vegetables such as:

Eggplant, sliced about ⅓-inch thick

Zucchini, sliced about ⅓-inch thick

Yellow squash, sliced about ⅓-inch thick

Portobello mushrooms, stems and gills removed but left whole

Button mushrooms, stems trimmed and left whole

Bell peppers, stemmed, seeded, and quartered

Asparagus, trimmed

Romaine lettuce, halved lengthwise (keep the core intact)

Red onion, sliced into ⅓-inch-thick rounds

Extra-virgin olive oil, for drizzling

Dressing

⅓ cup extra-virgin olive oil

3 tablespoons good vinegar (I prefer red wine vinegar)

2 tablespoons finely chopped fresh Italian parsley

2 tablespoons finely chopped fresh mint (optional)

1 tablespoon capers, rinsed and drained

2 garlic cloves, minced

Kosher salt and freshly ground black pepper

Verdura
a Brace

For this recipe we're going back to Tuscany once again because for almost every meal, whether we were eating in the villa or out at restaurants, we were served a big, beautiful platter of grilled vegetables. We're talking every kind of veg—mushrooms, zucchini, eggplant, tomatoes, lettuce (yes, lettuce!)—truly anything that was growing at the time. Now, I don't think a vegetable needs much more than some good char on the grill, a drizzle of olive oil, and salt to be delicious, but after eating these, I realized that if you also sprinkle on some vinegar, garlic, and capers, those vegetables' natural flavors really go to the next level. It's a particularly great use for all those vegetables that you grab at the market and don't have a clear plan for or that have been sitting in the fridge a bit too long. . . .

❋ *Make the grilled vegetables:* Preheat the grill to medium-high heat.

❋ In a large bowl or on a baking sheet, toss all the vegetables with just enough olive oil to coat. Lay the vegetables in a single layer on the grill and cook until the first side has developed nice, charred grill marks, 3 to 4 minutes. Flip to the second side and again cook until nice and charred, another 3 to 4 minutes. Bear in mind that depending on the type and thickness of your vegetables, they may need slightly more or less time, so keep an eye on them. Transfer the cooked vegetables to a serving platter and set aside.

❋ *Make the dressing:* In a small bowl, whisk together the oil, vinegar, parsley, mint (if using), capers, and garlic plus a pinch of salt and pepper.

❋ Drizzle the dressing over the vegetables and give everything a final pinch of salt. Allow the vegetables to sit for about 30 minutes before serving so they have time to come to room temperature and soak up that dressing.

NOTE

To roast the vegetables in the oven, spread them over a baking sheet or two, toss with just enough olive oil to coat, and cook at 425°F for 30 to 45 minutes, until tender and beginning to caramelize.

Grilled Peach & BURRATA SALAD

Italians love cooking with stone fruit. And one of the ways we like to do that is to grill the fruit to intensify its sweetness, then pair it with mild, creamy burrata, a handful of arugula, and a tangy olive oil dressing. It screams "special" and "expensive," but in reality, it's so simple and you get a lot of mileage out of just one ounce of burrata. This would be a perfect way to start a meal, or to serve alongside any other dish you'd be making in the summertime when stone fruit is in season.

❅ Preheat the grill to medium-high heat or a grill pan over medium-high heat on the stove.

❅ Halve each peach and remove the pit, then gently slice into quarters. Toss the pieces with 1 tablespoon of the olive oil. Lay the peach wedges in a single layer on the grill or grill pan and cook until they develop good char lines on each side, about 4 minutes total. Transfer them to a plate and set aside to cool slightly. Or let them cool completely, if you plan to serve them later.

❅ In a small jar, add the remaining 4 tablespoons oil, vinegar, chives, and honey. Season with a pinch of salt and pepper, seal the jar and give everything a good shake.

❅ To assemble the salad, place the burrata in the middle of a shallow bowl or platter. Arrange the grilled peaches, arugula, and tomatoes around the burrata and drizzle everything with the vinaigrette. Season with a light sprinkle of salt, scatter the basil over the top, and serve.

4 ripe but firm peaches (see Note)

5 tablespoons extra-virgin olive oil

2 tablespoons balsamic vinegar

2 tablespoons finely minced fresh chives

2 teaspoons honey

Kosher salt and freshly ground black pepper

1 (8-ounce) ball of burrata or 2 smaller ones

2 handfuls baby arugula

Handful of cherry or grape tomatoes, halved

7 or 8 small fresh basil leaves

NOTE

You could use a mix of fruit instead of just peaches. Other stone fruit such as cherries, apricots, and plums would also be delightful grilled and tossed in. If you can find peaches and plums at the same time, that's my favorite combination and the ultimate treat.

Zucchini *a Scapece*

5 small zucchini (about 1½ pounds), sliced into thin rounds

¼ cup extra-virgin olive oil

1 garlic clove, smashed and peeled

Kosher salt

3 tablespoons red wine vinegar

2 tablespoons chopped fresh mint

NOTE

If the zucchini hasn't browned after 20 minutes, pop 'em under the broiler for a few minutes.

If you go to the Amalfi coast in the summer, you're going to find an abundance of zucchini a scapece because you're going to find an abundance of zucchini, which grows like crazy there. It also happens to be the essence of simple, effortless warm weather cooking that delivers a big, flavorful result. In this dish, roasted zucchini takes a soak with olive oil, vinegar, and mint, making for a sharp, bright, fresh dish that can balance out something heavier on the table. It also happens to get even better the next day. Impossible to improve upon!

✳ Preheat the oven to 475°F.

✳ Line a baking sheet with parchment paper. Add the zucchini and toss to coat with the olive oil. Spread the zucchini in a single layer (if a few overlap, it's okay) and roast for 15 to 20 minutes (see Note), until crisp around the edges and golden brown on the bottom.

✳ Add the warm zucchini to a shallow bowl with the garlic, a pinch of salt, vinegar, and mint. Toss to combine and let the zucchini cool to room temperature for serving, about 10 minutes.

Creamy POLENTA

SERVES 4 TO 6

I've always said that polenta is like the Italian version of mashed potatoes. It's the ultimate rich, creamy comfort food, in addition to being the most versatile, satisfying side. Serving osso buco? There's gotta be polenta. Spezzatino with peas? Polenta. Grilled vegetables, fish, melanzane a funghetti? Polenta, polenta, polenta. It's fantastic under peperonata, and you have to serve it alongside my sautéed escarole once or twice in your life. And of course it can also stand on its own with nothing but some frizzled mushrooms, which are an easy addition that makes the polenta feel like a complete, delicious meal. Just one bowlful and you'll see why it transports me back to cozy afternoons in front of the fireplace with my nonno roasting chestnuts and my nonna sitting in her rocking chair.

✳ In a large saucepan, combine the stock and milk and bring to a gentle boil over medium-low heat. Slowly whisk in the polenta and cook, whisking often, until the polenta is soft and smooth, about 30 minutes. This is not something you want to wander too far away from; the polenta will thicken and bubble quite a bit as it cooks, and you don't want to risk it scorching on the bottom (be sure to get into those pan corners with a whisk or wooden spoon).

✳ Stir in the Parm and butter and season with salt and pepper to taste. Remove the pot from the heat and allow the polenta to sit for 5 minutes before serving. Just that small window is enough time for the polenta to go from slightly runny to thick and creamy—like food magic.

✳ Serve the polenta with frizzled mushrooms, if desired.

2 cups low-sodium chicken or vegetable stock

1½ cups whole milk

⅔ cup polenta (not quick-cooking)

¼ cup freshly grated Parmigiano-Reggiano cheese

1 tablespoon unsalted butter

Kosher salt and freshly ground black pepper

Frizzled Mushrooms (recipe follows), for serving (optional)

NOTE

Polenta loves creamy things; it wants to be boiled in stock and milk and finished with lots of butter, Parm, and black pepper or else it's bland. So give the polenta what it wants!

Recipe continues

Frizzled Mushrooms

SERVES 4

¼ cup extra-virgin olive oil

24 ounces mixed mushrooms (I like cremini, oyster, shiitake, and porcini, if you can find them)

Kosher salt and freshly ground black pepper

¼ cup chopped fresh Italian parsley

4 garlic cloves, thinly sliced

2 tablespoons unsalted butter

Serve these heaped over Creamy Polenta (page 221) or bruschetta with some Whipped Ricotta (page 42), or alongside Roasted Chicken (page 145), Veal Scaloppine (page 79), or pretty much any other main dish.

In a large skillet, heat the oil over medium heat (right between medium and medium-high is the sweet spot). When the oil begins to shimmer, add the mushrooms along with a pinch of salt and a couple cracks of pepper. Cook, stirring occasionally, until the mushrooms cook down and release their liquid, and then dry out, develop some color, and crisp around the edges, 10 to 15 minutes.

Add the parsley, garlic, and butter and cook for 1 more minute, stirring until fragrant. Remove the pan from the heat and serve.

FREGOLA
with Herbs & Pine Nuts

Kosher salt

1 cup fregola

½ cup chopped fresh
Italian parsley

¼ cup finely chopped
fresh mint (optional)

¼ cup finely minced fresh
chives

¼ cup extra-virgin
olive oil

Juice of 1 lemon

1 garlic clove, smashed
and peeled

Freshly ground black
pepper

¼ cup pine nuts, toasted in
a dry pan until fragrant

Fregola is a grain/pasta mash-up from Sardinia, where it's often served as a side. It's small balls of dough made with durum wheat semolina flour that have been toasted, giving them a nice nutty flavor and chewy pearl-couscous-like texture that's incredible by itself when cooked in some broth with Parmigiana. Fregola also makes a great accompaniment because it doesn't compete with other flavors; it just enhances them. I wanted to have an herby moment somewhere in this book, so I call for folding in tons of fresh parsley, chives, and mint plus lemon juice, garlic, and toasted pine nuts. It's the kind of back-pocket dish you can reach for to go with steak, chicken, or vegetables. It also gets better the longer it sits, so I like making enough to have for lunch the next day, especially with a hard-boiled egg on top.

✳ Fill a large pot with water, add a generous pinch of salt, and bring to a boil over medium-high heat. Cook the fregola to al dente according to the package directions, usually 9 to 11 minutes.

✳ Meanwhile, in a large bowl, combine the parsley, mint (if using), chives, olive oil, lemon juice, and garlic. Set aside.

✳ When the fregola is ready, reserve ¼ cup of the cooking water before draining the fregola and shocking it under cold water to stop the cooking process. You want the fregola to be warm but not hot (or cold).

✳ Add the fregola and the reserved cooking water to the bowl with the herbs and season to taste with salt and pepper. Cover with plastic wrap and allow it to sit at room temperature for 30 minutes. Sprinkle with the pine nuts and serve.

*(Because No *Self-Respecting* ITALIAN Would DARE Have a *Special* Meal Without One) *

SWEET ENDINGS

MAYBE IT'S THE ITALIAN *in me, maybe* it's just good sense, but if there's a "special meal"—meaning pretty much anything that's not served on the fly while life is going at full speed (though sometimes then, too)—there's gotta be dessert. Full stop. But I didn't grow up eating cupcakes, chocolate chip cookies, and ice cream sundaes. No, when I think of a sweet treat, I think about spongy, pudding-like semolina cake, lighter-than-air fried dough, and of course, strawberries soaked in limoncello. These are the recipes that I am reaching for to ensure that no one gets up from my table without a very full, happy belly. They're also what I'm bringing to people's houses whenever I'm being hosted, what I gift for the holidays or to say Thank You, and what I'm making with Mia any chance I can because there's no memories like those formed over freshly fried chiacchiere , a slice of Nonna's fruit crostata, or a mug of Italian hot chocolate so thick you need to eat it with a spoon.

They're also the recipes that I feel the most strongly about preserving the tradition of because they are the dishes that my nonna grew up eating and learning to make. Most of them are regional Neapolitan specialties that have been passed down for generations by women who cook and bake like my grandma—meaning they never got the memo that baking is a science and you have to, you know, *measure*. For Nonna, baking, like cooking, has always been about look and feel, never exact measures. The recipes that I did manage to find in her house had been scribbled on napkins and scraps of paper saying things like "a little bit of flour" or "a ton of eggs." To have spent the time lovingly and carefully piecing together each of these recipes with her and then sharing them with you is just as special as the dishes themselves. So, for those of you who have been searching for them like the little treasures that they are, here you go! And for the rest of you, now you'll know to have a dessert anytime Nonna comes over, or else she'll be talking about you on the whole way home. She's sassy, but we love her. ❋

Nonna's CROSTATA di Frutta

Crust

1½ cups all-purpose flour, plus more for dusting and rolling

1 stick (4 ounces) cold unsalted butter, cubed into small pieces

2 tablespoons sugar

⅛ teaspoon kosher salt

1 large egg

2 tablespoons cold water

Custard

2½ cups whole milk

Zest of ½ lemon (a vegetable peeler works well here)

1 vanilla bean, split lengthwise

4 large egg yolks

¼ cup sugar

¼ cup all-purpose flour

2 tablespoons cornstarch

⅛ teaspoon kosher salt

This recipe is first up because it's my nonna's most-baked dessert and also her most famous. I was once out to dinner and someone came by the table just to tell me that they had to go visit Nonna sometime soon just so he could have her crostata. What can I tell you, it's everyone's favorite and for good reason. This tart is light, delicious, scented with lemon and oranges, enriched with vanilla custard, and full of whatever fruit is in season. It would be right at home as part of a brunch spread, will complement anything you're serving for dinner, or can be a perfectly respectable snack. Do note that it's best to let the tart set up for a few hours (or overnight) before serving.

✳ *Make the crust:* In a food processor, combine the flour, butter, sugar, and salt and pulse 10 to 15 times, until the butter is evenly distributed in the dry ingredients and there aren't any pieces larger than a small pea. Add the egg and water and pulse just until the mixture comes together when pinched between your fingers.

✳ Turn the dough out onto a lightly floured work surface and pull it together into a mound. Press into a disk, wrap in plastic wrap, and refrigerate for at least 45 minutes or up to overnight.

✳ *Meanwhile, make the custard:* In a medium saucepan, combine the milk and lemon zest. With the tip of a knife, scrape the vanilla seeds into the pan and add the pod, too. Bring to a simmer over medium-low heat, then reduce to the lowest setting and gently simmer until the milk thickens and coats the back of a spoon, about 10 minutes. Remove the pot from the heat (discard the lemon zest and vanilla pod).

✳ In a medium bowl, combine the egg yolks and sugar. Use a hand mixer to beat the mixture for about 2 minutes, until light and frothy. (You could also do this in a stand mixer fitted with the whisk.) Add the flour, cornstarch, and salt and whisk for 1 more minute. (It will seem thick at first—that's normal.) While continuing to mix, stream in half of the hot milk mixture.

✳ Pour the egg yolk mixture into the saucepan and, whisking constantly, cook over low heat until you can drag your finger down the back of your spoon and the line will remain, about 5 minutes. Transfer the mixture to a medium bowl, cover with plastic wrap, and set aside at room temperature while you assemble the crostata.

✳ *Assemble the crostata:* Preheat the oven to 375°F. Butter a 9-inch tart pan with a removable bottom.

✳ Take the dough out of the fridge and allow it to sit at room temperature for 5 minutes, or until it softens just enough to roll out (it may take a touch longer if you've left it overnight). On a lightly floured surface, use a rolling pin to roll the dough into a roughly 12-inch round. It's okay if it tears here and there; just pinch the pieces back together. Carefully lift the dough into the prepared tart pan and press it into the fluted sides, pinching off any excess at the pan edge. (I encourage you to save the scraps for later; see Note.)

✳ Pierce the bottom of the crust all over with a fork, then lay a sheet of parchment paper over the top. Fill the crust with pie weights (or dried beans or rice) and bake for 15 minutes. Carefully remove the parchment and weights and bake until the edges and bottom are lightly golden, another 10 minutes. Allow the crust to cool completely.

✳ Meanwhile, in a small microwave-safe bowl, combine the jam with 2 teaspoons water and microwave until runny, about 15 seconds. Set aside.

✳ Fill the cooled crust with the custard (give it a good stir to loosen it up first), then top with the fruit. Brush the apricot mixture over the top, loosely cover with plastic wrap, and refrigerate for at least 6 hours before serving, or up to overnight.

Assembly

Softened unsalted butter for the tart pan

2 tablespoons apricot jam

2 to 3 cups fresh fruit of choice (my favorite combination is strawberries, peeled and sliced kiwi, and blackberries)

NOTE

If you saved the dough scraps, you can gather them up, roll them out to about ¼ inch thick, and bake on a baking sheet at 375°F until golden, about 10 minutes. Sprinkle with some powdered sugar and enjoy as a cook's treat!

Nonna's Crostata di Frutta ✳ *page 230*

Zeppole San Giuseppe ✳ *page 234*

ZEPPOLE
San Giuseppe

Custard

2½ cups whole milk

Grated zest of ½ lemon

1 vanilla bean, split lengthwise

4 large egg yolks

¼ cup granulated sugar

4 tablespoons all-purpose flour

2 tablespoon cornstarch

⅛ teaspoon kosher salt

Zeppole

1 stick (4 ounces) unsalted butter

3 tablespoons granulated sugar

Grated zest of ½ lemon

¼ teaspoon kosher salt

1 cup all-purpose flour

3 large eggs

1 tablespoon limoncello (optional), homemade (page 265) or store-bought

To Finish

Vegetable or canola oil (if deep-frying)

1 large egg

Amarena cherries (see Note)

Powdered sugar

March 19 is an important date in Italy because it's St. Joseph's Day, and it also happens to be when we celebrate Father's Day. As part of the festivities, we have zeppole San Giuseppe, which if you were to walk into pretty much any house in Naples, you'd find on the table. Now, being married to a Joseph, there's not a March 19 that goes by without me making a batch of these super-light, rich-but-not-too-rich, custard-filled, Amarena cherry–topped fritters. I always serve them as any self-respecting Italian woman would: with a shot of ice-cold grappa and frozen Concord grapes, which you can always find in my freezer.

✳ *Make the custard:* In a medium saucepan, stir together the milk, lemon zest, and salt. Use the tip of a knife to scrape in the vanilla seeds and also add the pod. Set over medium-low heat and bring to a gentle simmer.

✳ Meanwhile, in a stand mixer fitted with the whisk (or in a large bowl with a hand mixer), whisk together the egg yolks and granulated sugar until thick and pale, about 2 minutes. Add the flour and cornstarch and whisk until combined. The mixture will be very thick at this point.

✳ Discard the vanilla pod from the milk mixture. While whisking the egg mixture, add about one-quarter of the hot milk mixture to it. Then transfer the entire mixture to the saucepan and return to medium-low heat. Stir constantly until the custard thickens to the point where if you drag your finger down the back of your spoon, the line will remain, 5 to 7 minutes.

✳ Remove the saucepan from the heat and transfer the custard to a bowl (strain if desired). Cover with plastic wrap, making sure that the wrap is touching the surface of the custard to prevent it from developing a "skin" on top. Pop it in the fridge to cool completely while you make the zeppole.

✳ *Make the zeppole:* In a large saucepan, combine 1 cup water, the butter, granulated sugar, lemon zest, and salt. Bring to a boil over medium-high heat, whisk in the flour, and continue whisking until the mixture starts pulling away from the sides of the pan and forming a ball, about 1 minute.

❋ Transfer the mixture to a stand mixer fitted with the paddle and mix on low speed for 2 minutes to help it cool slightly. One at a time, add the eggs, mixing well after each addition. Add the limoncello (if using) and mix until the dough is uniform and smooth, about 2 minutes.

❋ *To finish:* From here you can either bake or fry the zeppole. I actually prefer baked, but you do you.

❋ If baking the zeppole, preheat the oven to 375°F. Line two sheet pans with parchment paper.

❋ If frying the zeppole, pour 3 to 4 inches of vegetable oil into a large heavy pot and heat over medium heat to 350°F. Cut out twelve 4-inch squares of parchment paper and lay them on a baking sheet. Line a large platter with paper towels.

❋ For both cooking methods, fit a piping bag with a ½-inch star tip and fill the bag with the zeppole dough. Pipe 12 nest-shape circles, 3 inches wide, with a 1¼-inch hole in the center. (If baking, be sure to leave a few inches between the zeppole so they have room to expand properly.)

❋ In a small bowl, whisk the egg with 1 tablespoon water. Brush the egg wash over each zeppole.

❋ If baking, bake until deeply golden brown, 30 to 40 minutes. Remove from the oven and allow to cool completely (right on the sheet pan is fine).

❋ If frying, add 2 zeppole to the hot oil with the parchment still attached (it will instantly peel itself away from the zeppole and you can use a spider to remove it from the oil). Cook until the first side is golden brown, about 2 minutes. Flip and repeat on the second side, about 4 minutes total. Transfer the cooked zeppole to the paper towels to cool while you repeat with the remaining zeppole.

❋ Once the zeppole have cooled completely, fit a clean piping bag with the star tip and fill the bag with the custard. Cut the zeppole in half horizontally. Pipe the custard over the bottom halves of the zeppole and replace the top halves. Top each with a cherry and finish with a sprinkling of powdered sugar. Serve immediately.

NOTE

I don't like asking people to buy special ingredients, but if you decided to just buy one, let it be good Amarena cherries, which are a small, bitter Italian cherry that's been preserved in syrup. Their slight bitterness really balances the richness of the custard and pastry.

AMARETTI & *Jam* CROSTATA

Crust

2 cups all-purpose flour, plus more as needed

¼ cup sugar

½ teaspoon baking powder

¼ teaspoon salt

1 stick (4 ounces) cold unsalted butter, cut into small pieces

2 teaspoons vanilla extract

Grated zest of ½ lemon

2 large eggs

Assembly

Softened butter for the pan

2 tablespoons amaretto, dark rum, or Marsala (amaretto is my favorite)

1 (10-ounce) jar apricot jam

About 30 amaretti cookies

1 large egg

1 tablespoon milk or water

1 tablespoon sugar

This simple crostata requires only a handful of simple pantry ingredients, but they are put together in such a way that they become more than the sum of their parts. Normally dry, crumbly amaretti transform into flavorful, spongy little pillows when soaked in amaretto or dark rum. They are then layered over sweet, sticky jam.

✳ *Make the crust:* In a food processor, combine the flour, sugar, baking powder, and salt and pulse to combine. Add the butter, vanilla, and lemon zest and pulse 15 times, or until the mixture looks like coarse sand. Add the eggs and pulse until the mixture comes together into a dough. Don't worry about overworking the butter!

✳ Turn the dough out onto a clean surface and knead it into a disc. You can dust with a little flour if you need to, but the dough should be pretty bouncy and smooth. Shape the dough into a disk, enclose it in plastic wrap, and refrigerate for 45 minutes or overnight.

✳ *Assemble the crostata:* Preheat the oven to 375°F. Butter a 9-inch cake pan. Remove the crust from the fridge and allow it to soften slightly at room temperature so it's easier to roll out.

✳ In a small bowl, mix together the amaretto with 2 tablespoons water and set aside.

✳ Cut two-thirds of the dough off the disk and use a rolling pin to roll it into a 14-inch round about ¼ inch thick. Carefully transfer the dough to the prepared pan, allowing the excess to drape over the edges.

✳ In a small microwave-safe bowl, microwave the jam for 20 seconds to loosen it slightly. Spread the jam over the crust. Dip each amaretti cookie into the amaretto mixture and set on top of the jam in a single layer until you can no longer fit any more.

Recipe continues

✳ Use a rolling pin to roll out the remaining piece of dough into a roughly 12-inch round about ¼ inch thick. Carefully transfer the dough over the top of the amaretti layer. Press the edges together and use a paring knife to trim the excess so there's still a little overhang to seal the top and bottom together. Crimp the edges and use a knife to pierce the top in several places.

✳ In a small bowl, whisk together the egg and milk. Brush the top of the crostata with the egg wash and sprinkle all over with the sugar.

✳ Bake until the crust is deeply golden, 20 to 25 minutes. Allow the crostata to cool before slicing and serving.

MIGLIACCIO
Napoletano

I suppose you could say that this semolina cake is the Italian version of a yellow cake. But it's not fluffy and light; it's spongy, moist, and almost pudding-y—somewhere between crème brûlée and cheesecake and scented with vanilla and citrus. When serving this at her house, my grandmother would make a quick batch of whipped cream and dollop that and boozy limoncello-soaked strawberries on top, which are a necessity, in my opinion. It could be a celebration cake, or just a cake that makes anything feel like a celebration. Either way, one piece of this, and you may never want to go back to basic yellow cake again.

✳ The night before, line a fine-mesh sieve with cheesecloth, spoon in the ricotta, and set it over a large bowl. Refrigerate and let it drain overnight.

✳ *Make the semolina:* In a large saucepan, combine the milk, butter, orange zest, lemon zest, and vanilla bean paste. Bring to a gentle simmer over medium-low heat and simmer until the butter has melted and the mixture is perfumed with citrus, about 5 minutes. While whisking, slowly stream in the semolina. Continue whisking until the mixture thickens slightly, about 2 minutes. Switch to a wooden spoon and continue stirring until the semolina thickens to the consistency of mashed potatoes, about 20 minutes. Remove the pot from the heat and set the semolina aside to cool to room temperature.

✳ Once cooled, remove the orange and lemon zest and discard. Transfer the semolina to a food processor and puree until smooth. (This might seem like an extra step, but it's key for getting that quintessential smooth, bouncy, somewhat custardy cake texture.) Set aside.

✳ *Make the cake:* Preheat the oven to 350°F. Line the bottom of a 9-inch springform pan with a round of parchment paper and lightly coat the sides with cooking spray.

1½ cups whole-milk ricotta cheese

Semolina
4½ cups whole milk

4 tablespoons unsalted butter

Zest of ½ orange (a vegetable peeler works well here)

Zest of ½ lemon (a vegetable peeler works well here)

1 teaspoon vanilla bean paste or vanilla extract

1¼ cups semolina flour

Cake
Cooking spray

1¼ cups sugar

5 large eggs

Grated zest of ½ orange

Grated zest of ½ lemon

½ teaspoon vanilla bean paste or vanilla extract

½ teaspoon kosher salt

Boozy Strawberries (page 264), for serving (optional, but strongly recommended)

Recipe continues

✳ In a large bowl with a hand mixer (or in a stand mixer fitted with the whisk), beat together the sugar, eggs, orange zest, lemon zest, and vanilla until thick and pale, about 2 minutes. Add the drained ricotta, salt, and pureed semolina and continue beating until well incorporated, 2 to 3 minutes.

✳ Pour the batter into the prepared pan and smooth the top. Bake until lightly golden around the edges and mostly set, about 1 hour. The center will have a bit of a jiggle when the side of the pan is tapped. The cake will set as it cools.

✳ Allow the cake to cool to room temperature, about 2 hours. Remove the sides of the pan and transfer the cake (still on the pan bottom) to the refrigerator for at least another 2 hours or up to overnight (which is what I like to do).

✳ If desired, serve topped with the boozy berries.

Torta CAPRESE

Softened butter
for the pan

8 ounces bittersweet
chocolate, preferably
Ghirardelli, chopped

2 sticks (8 ounces)
unsalted butter, cut into
tablespoon-size pieces

5 large eggs, separated

1 cup granulated sugar

2 teaspoons vanilla
extract

1¾ cups almond flour

¼ teaspoon kosher salt

Powdered sugar, for
dusting

Whenever Mia and I want to bake something decadent, this is always at the top of the list. And it never fails to remind me of every summer when my family would spend a few weeks up the coast in Mondragone visiting my aunt Zia Maria—it was a sure bet that she'd make the best chocolate cake. My cousins, Angela and Gina, and I would be in the kitchen helping her, and as our reward, she'd give us espresso spoons with batter to lick while we waited for the cake to come out of the oven—a tradition that Mia would agree has stood the test of time. Eventually we'd be treated to the most deeply fudgy chocolate cake you can imagine, topped with the thickest layer of powdered sugar. It's a classic cake from Capri, and while I've never had it there, I have to think Zia Maria—and this recipe—have done it justice.

✳ Preheat the oven to 350°F. Butter the sides and bottom of a 9-inch springform pan.

✳ In a small microwave-safe bowl, combine the chocolate and butter. Microwave in 30-second increments, stirring after each, until the chocolate and butter are melted. Set aside to cool.

✳ In a medium bowl with a hand mixer (or in a stand mixer fitted with the whisk), beat the egg whites until they form stiff peaks, 4 to 5 minutes. Set aside. (Or transfer to another bowl, if using a stand mixer.)

✳ In a large bowl with a hand mixer (or in a stand mixer fitted with the whisk), beat together the egg yolks, granulated sugar, and vanilla until the mixture becomes thick and pale in color, about 2 minutes. Add the chocolate/butter mixture and continue whisking to combine. Add the almond flour and salt and whisk until well incorporated.

✳ Using a spatula, gently fold the egg whites into the batter, one-quarter at a time, being careful to not deflate them. The batter will be quite thick at first, and that's okay! Once all of the egg whites have been folded into the batter and no streaks remain, carefully transfer the batter to the prepared pan, spreading it out evenly but taking care to not deflate it.

⁜ Bake until firm around the edges with a tiny bit of jiggle in the center, about 40 minutes. Transfer to a rack to cool completely in the pan.

⁜ Once cooled, run a knife around the edges of the cake, release the pan sides and remove from the cake. Transfer the torta (still on the bottom of the pan) to a serving platter. Dust with powdered sugar and serve.

CREMA DI CAFFÈ
(aka Cheat Tiramisu)

¼ cup brewed espresso, chilled

2 tablespoons powdered sugar

1 cup heavy cream

Unsweetened cocoa powder, for dusting (optional)

My nonna always had a stash of leftover espresso and heavy cream in the fridge and powdered sugar on hand, making it easy to quickly whip this up for unexpected company or us grandkids. She'd serve it in a little espresso cup with a little espresso spoon, and you knew that with a cup of crema di caffè in front of you, everything was going to be okay. Now that I'm the kind of person who leaves coffee behind in the pot and reheats it all day, I can continue this tradition (and my little sister loves me for it). I've also discovered that if you throw it into the freezer for an hour and a half, it develops a semifreddo-like texture. Served with a side of brioche (something we Italians love with our ice cream), it's bliss.

✳ In a small bowl, stir together the coffee and sugar and set aside.

✳ In a large bowl with a hand mixer (or in a stand mixer fitted with the whisk)—or in an empty screw-top jar that all your kids/grandkids can take turns shaking, if you want to do it Nonna-style—whisk the cream on medium-high speed until it develops stiff peaks, a couple of minutes. Drizzle in the coffee mixture and continue whisking until stiff peaks form. Cover with plastic wrap and refrigerate for 1 hour. (I don't recommend holding it longer than that or the cream will start to separate.)

✳ Serve in mugs, if desired, dusting the top with cocoa powder.

HAZELNUT
Semifreddo

I discovered this dessert years ago when visiting the Amalfi Coast and stumbling upon a restaurant called Trattoria da Lorenzo. It's one of the happiest accidents of my life because what I assumed would be a tourist trap turned out to have some of the best food I'd ever eaten. After I went there a few times and made friends with the owner, he brought out a big board full of all their delicious desserts—and this was one of them. It is essentially the richest, most velvety ice cream/cake batter mash-up topped with salted hazelnut brittle and a pinch of sea salt. And for the love of all that's holy, it was perhaps the best ice cream bite I've had in my life. So of course I had to figure out how to make it at home, which I do any time I want to think of warm, sunny days at da Lorenzo, or I want to treat my family to something extra special after a long week.

❊ *Make the semifreddo:* Fill a small saucepan with about 2 inches of water and bring to a boil over medium-high heat. Reduce to a simmer.

❊ In a medium heatproof bowl that can sit over the saucepan, whisk together the egg yolks, sugar, and salt until the mixture becomes thick and pale in color, about 3 minutes. Place the bowl on top of the saucepan and continue whisking until the mixture is thick enough to coat the back of a spoon, about 10 minutes.

❊ Whisk in the hazelnut liqueur and vanilla. Set a fine-mesh sieve over a medium bowl and strain the mixture into the bowl (this is to remove any bits of cooked egg, so don't skip it). Cover the custard with plastic wrap, making sure the plastic is gently pressed against the top so a skin doesn't form. Refrigerate for at least 3 hours or up to 24 hours.

❊ Once the custard is nice and cold, in a bowl with a hand mixer or whisk (or in a stand mixer fitted with the whisk), whip or whisk the cream until stiff peaks form. Use a spatula to fold the whipped cream into the chilled custard, then transfer the mixture to the canister of an ice cream machine or other container with a tight-fitting lid and freeze overnight.

Semifreddo

7 large egg yolks

⅔ cup sugar

¼ teaspoon kosher salt

¼ cup hazelnut liqueur

1 tablespoon vanilla bean paste or pure vanilla extract

1½ cups heavy cream

Hazelnut Praline

1 cup peeled hazelnuts

1 tablespoon sesame seeds (optional)

1¼ cups sugar

Flaky sea salt (I like Maldon)

Recipe continues

Fair warning: If you skip the salted hazelnut praline, you'll have a delicious dessert, but I'm sorry to say that your life will not be complete.

✴ *Make the hazelnut praline:* Do this a few hours from serving. In a large dry skillet, toast the hazelnuts over medium-low heat, shaking the pan occasionally to ensure they toast evenly, until they are lightly brown all over, about 5 minutes. During the last 30 seconds, add the sesame seeds (if using) and frequently shake the pan. Remove the pan from the heat.

✴ Line a baking sheet with parchment paper and have at the ready. In a medium saucepan, combine the sugar and ¼ cup water. Bring to a boil over medium-low heat, swirling the pan occasionally (do not be tempted to stir), and continue boiling until the mixture turns a deep amber color, about 10 minutes. Remove the pan from the heat, quickly stir in the toasted nuts, and carefully pour the mixture onto the prepared baking sheet (the sugar is very hot—take extra care to be safe). Sprinkle the brittle with flaky salt. Allow the praline to cool and harden, about 1 hour.

✴ Break the praline into large chunks and add them to a food processor. Pulse until the praline forms crystal-like sprinkles. Transfer to a small bowl and set aside.

✴ About 15 minutes before serving, take the semifreddo out of the freezer to come to room temperature. Scoop into dessert glasses and sprinkle with a generous amount of praline.

PASTIERA *Napoletana*

MAKES TWO 9-INCH PIES

Traditionally this citrus-scented grain and ricotta pie is made only once a year, for Easter, but it's way too special for that to be it. I always asked Nonna to make it for my birthday, and now I also make one for Christmas (especially because it falls so close to my birthday). I also make a few extras to give away as presents . . . in addition to the one I make for myself and freeze in individual pieces so I can enjoy a slice whenever I'm feeling homesick or upset or simply want to enjoy a sweet treat by myself. Yes, it's a little bit of a labor of love because in addition to making a crust and ricotta filling you need to babysit a pot of simmering grano cotto (cooked wheat). And yes, you have to make it ahead so it can be served cold. And yes, I have asked that you track down a couple specialty ingredients (like millefiori, a "thousand flowers" extract that you can find in an Italian grocery or online). But I assure you that it's worth it. This pie changes lives.

Grano

1 (580-gram) jar grano cotto (see Notes)

3½ cups whole milk

4 tablespoons unsalted butter

Crust

4 cups all-purpose flour

2 sticks (8 ounces) unsalted butter, cut into cubes

½ cup sugar

½ teaspoon kosher salt

Grated zest of ½ orange (see Notes)

Grated zest of ½ lemon (see Notes)

4 large egg yolks

¼ to ½ cup ice water

2 teaspoons vanilla extract

Cook the grano: In a large saucepan or soup pot (nonstick is best for this), combine the grano, milk, and butter. Bring the mixture to a boil over medium heat. Reduce the heat to low and simmer, stirring often, for 3 hours. At first it will look like a curdled mess, but trust the process! The grano will swell and soften, and the mixture will be thick.

Remove the pan from the heat and immediately cover with plastic wrap, making sure it is touching the surface of the grano. Allow the mixture to come to room temperature, then pop into the fridge for 2 hours to cool completely.

Meanwhile, make the crust: In a stand mixer fitted with the paddle, combine the flour, butter, sugar, salt, orange zest, and lemon zest. Mix until the butter is in pea-size pieces and is evenly distributed throughout the mixture. Add the egg yolks, ¼ cup of the ice water, and the vanilla and mix until the mixture comes together into a dough. If you pinch the dough between your fingers and it crumbles, add more water, 1 tablespoon at a time, until it holds together. Don't worry about overmixing. We aren't going for a flaky crust here; it will be a bit denser, like a tart dough.

Recipe continues

Filling and Assembly

Cooking spray

6 large eggs

1½ cups sugar

1 pound fresh whole-milk ricotta cheese

½ cup candied citrus peel, very finely chopped

Grated zest of ½ orange

Grated zest of ½ lemon

½ teaspoon millefiori extract (see Notes)

¼ teaspoon ground cinnamon

All-purpose flour, for dusting

NOTES

Grano cotto is a cooked wheat grain that's sold in jars in Italian markets and online. And yes, we cook it a second time to make the pastiera.

For the orange zest and lemon zest, grate a whole orange and a whole lemon and divide in two: half for the crust and half for the filling.

The millefiori extract you can also find in an Italian market or online.

✴ Shape the dough into a rectangle and cover with plastic wrap. Refrigerate for 1 hour.

✴ *Make the filling and assemble the pies:* Preheat the oven to 375°F. Lightly coat two 9-inch round cake pans with cooking spray.

✴ In a very large bowl, whisk together the eggs and sugar. Add the ricotta, chopped candied peel, orange zest, lemon zest, millefiori, and cinnamon and whisk to combine. Use a wooden spoon to stir in the cooled grano mixture until everything is well combined. Set aside.

✴ Lightly flour a clean work surface. Cut off one-quarter of the rectangle of dough and set aside. Divide the remaining dough in half, shape each into a disk, then use a rolling pin to roll out each into a 12-inch round, dusting with more flour as needed. Carefully transfer the dough to the prepared pans, gently pressing it into the bottom and trimming any overhanging dough. Divide the filling between the two pans and set aside.

✴ Shape the reserved dough into a disk and roll it out into a 10-inch round, again dusting with more flour if the dough begins to stick. Cut the round into strips ½ inch wide. Use half the strips to create a lattice pattern on the first pie, pinching the end of each strip with the edge of the crust, then trimming off any excess. Repeat with the second pie.

✴ Bake the pies until deeply golden brown, about 1 hour. Allow the pies to cool at room temperature, then cover with foil and refrigerate overnight, or for up to 4 days, before serving.

Thick ITALIAN Hot Chocolate

MAKES 4
TEACUP-SIZE
SERVINGS
OR 8 ESPRESSO-SIZE
SERVINGS
*(which I prefer because
this is so rich)*

When I got to the States, I didn't know that you could *drink* hot chocolate, because in Italy it's eaten with a spoon. The reason why this recipe lives here, though, is not because creamy, decadent hot chocolate that's too thick to drink is one of the most delicious treats you could have when it's cold. No, it's because it pays homage to my mom's mom and her neighbor Signora Maria, who every year on Santo Antonio, her son's name day, would make this for all the kids in the neighborhood. It would be perfectly bitter and sweet and there'd be homemade cookies for dipping. Thirty years later, she's still doing it, and there's not a January that goes by that I don't do the same for my daughter and her friends.

✳ In a small saucepan, whisk together the milk, sugar, cocoa powder, and cornstarch. Place the pot over low heat and cook, stirring constantly, until the mixture comes to a light boil and thickens, about 5 minutes. Remove the pot from the heat and add the chocolate and the salt. Whisk until the chocolate has melted.

✳ Divide the hot chocolate among your cups of choice and serve with shortbread cookies for dunking.

2 cups whole milk

¼ cup sugar

¼ cup unsweetened cocoa powder (I like Hershey's Cocoa Special Dark/100% Cacao), sifted

4 teaspoons cornstarch (see Notes)

4 ounces dark chocolate (I like Ghirardelli bittersweet/60% cacao), broken into pieces (see Notes)

Pinch of kosher salt

Shortbread cookies, for serving

NOTES

If you prefer a drinkable version of this hot cocoa, omit the cornstarch.

You could use semisweet or milk chocolate instead of bittersweet.

PASTICCIOTTI

Crust

1½ cups all-purpose flour

1 stick (4 ounces) cold unsalted butter, cut into small pieces

2 tablespoons sugar

⅛ teaspoon kosher salt

1 large egg

2 tablespoons cold water

Custard

1¼ cups whole milk

Zest of ½ lemon (a vegetable peeler works well here)

1 vanilla bean, split lengthwise

2 large egg yolks

2 tablespoons sugar

2 tablespoons all-purpose flour

1 tablespoon cornstarch

⅛ teaspoon kosher salt

Pasticciotti means "a mess," because this recipe is the result of just that, or more accurately, leftovers. It takes extra pie dough plus extra custard from making a crostata (like the one on page 230) and combines them into scrumptious little pocket tarts. They're Mia's favorite, favorite treat, and I love making them when it's chilly out, because they're best enjoyed warm out of the oven; plus, they make the house smell so inviting and cozy. There are no hard or fast rules about how to make them, either. You could use a little brioche mold, but I like a muffin tin because I value my sanity. If the custard bubbles out? Even better. They're meant to be messy and imperfect—which also makes them the ideal recipes for letting the kids help you. And once you try them, you'll understand why Nonna would always double her pie dough and custard recipes just so she'd have an excuse to make pasticciotti.

✳ *Make the crust:* In a food processor, combine the flour, butter, sugar, and salt. Pulse 10 to 15 times, or until the butter is evenly distributed among the dry ingredients. Add the egg and water and pulse until the mixture comes together when pinched between your fingers.

✳ Turn the dough out onto a clean work surface and gather it into a disk. Enclose in plastic wrap and refrigerate for 45 minutes.

✳ *Meanwhile, make the custard:* In a small saucepan, combine the milk and lemon zest. With the tip of a sharp knife, scrape the vanilla seeds into the pan and add the vanilla pod. Bring to a simmer over medium heat. Keep on a low simmer (as low as it goes) for 10 minutes, then remove from the heat. Remove and discard the lemon zest and vanilla pod.

✳ In a medium bowl, whisk together the egg yolks and sugar until light and frothy (I like using a hand mixer for this), about 2 minutes. Add the flour, cornstarch, and salt and whisk for 1 more minute. The mixture will seem thick at first, but that's normal. Continue whisking as you stream in half of the hot milk mixture.

Recipe continues

Assembly

**Baking spray (I like
Baker's Joy)**

**All-purpose flour,
for dusting**

1 large egg

**1 tablespoon whole milk
or water**

2 tablespoons sugar

⁜ Return the egg yolk and milk mixture to the saucepan with the remaining milk and set over low heat. Whisk constantly until the mixture is thick enough to coat the back of a spoon, about 5 minutes. Transfer the mixture to a bowl, cover with plastic wrap, and set aside at room temperature while you finish assembling the pasticciotti.

⁜ *To assemble:* When the dough is done chilling, let it sit at room temperature for about 5 minutes until it softens just enough to roll out. In the meantime, grease 12 cups of a muffin tin with baking spray.

⁜ Lightly flour a clean work surface and use a rolling pin to roll out the dough ¼ inch thick. Use a 4½-inch round cookie or biscuit cutter to cut out 12 rounds. Add each to the prepared muffin cups; they'll come only about halfway up the sides. Gather the dough scraps into a disk, cover with plastic wrap, and pop it into the freezer for 5 minutes to chill before rolling it out again.

⁜ Once again roll out the dough to ¼ inch thick, then use a round cutter that's slightly smaller than 4 inches so the rounds fit perfectly on top of the pasticciotti.

⁜ In a small bowl, whisk together the egg and milk. Spoon about 1 tablespoon custard into each muffin cup, then brush the edges of the bottom piece of dough with the egg wash and add a top. Press the tines of a fork into the edges to seal the sides, then brush the top with egg wash. Sprinkle the pasticciotti with sugar (just a tiny bit) and freeze for 10 minutes.

⁜ Meanwhile, preheat the oven to 375°F.

⁜ Bake the pasticciotti until golden brown, 20 to 25 minutes. Allow them to cool only slightly before serving (I find using a fork to help gently lift them out works well). They're best eaten warm.

Prosecco SORBET FIZZ

I was once invited to a very fabulous, very extravagant party in Italy, at the end of which we were all served Prosecco with a little scoop of sorbet at the bottom of the glass. Prosecco is like the Sprite of all things celebratory for Italians—they're popping and pouring for anything and everything—but if that adorable pastel scoop at the bottom doesn't define *festive*, I don't know what does. Ever since, I've been making this for any bubbles-worthy occasion—which, if you know me, is pretty much anytime. It's an ideal accompaniment for starters and snacks or the end of a meal; it's appropriate for fancy dinners or hanging with the girls; it's like sipping Tuscany or Amalfi Coast sunshine; and it's as low effort (more like *no* effort) as it gets.

✦ Add a 2-ounce scoop of sorbet to each Champagne flute, top with Prosecco, garnish with mint, and enjoy right away!

1 pint sorbet (I love mango, raspberry, melon, and, of course, my Sorbetto al Limone, page 262)

1 (750 ml) bottle good Prosecco

Sprigs fresh mint, for garnish

Chiacchiere

1½ cups plus
2 tablespoons all-purpose
flour, plus more for
dusting

2 tablespoons granulated
sugar

½ teaspoon baking
powder

¼ teaspoon salt

2 tablespoons unsalted
butter, at room
temperature

2 large eggs

¼ cup white wine (pinot
grigio for me, always)

Grated zest of ½ lemon

Vegetable or canola oil,
for frying

Powdered sugar, for
serving

This is a classic cookie that you find in Naples during Carnivale, which is like our Halloween because everyone dresses up and eats sweets. Made from a thin almost pasta dough–like pastry (which includes white wine to make them light, crisp, and slightly puffed), these get fried until golden brown and then are coated in powdered sugar. They are a welcome little treat at the end of a meal and are quite the showstopper if you pull out your portable skillet (page 20) and make them fresh. To get the dough nice and thin, I use a pasta machine, because I haven't quite nailed Nonna's rolling technique. Somehow, she's able to get the dough super thin without it tearing, but I'm not that lucky, so a pasta roller it is.

✳ In a stand mixer fitted with the dough hook, add the flour, sugar, baking powder, and salt. Mix on low speed just to combine. Add the butter and mix on low for another minute, then add the eggs, wine, and lemon zest. Knead until the mixture comes together into a soft dough that holds together, about 3 minutes.

✳ Lightly flour a clean work surface and turn out the dough. Knead the dough by hand for a few minutes, adding more flour if the dough gets sticky, until the dough is smooth. Shape the dough into a ball, enclose in plastic wrap, and allow it to rest for 45 minutes at room temperature.

✳ Lightly flour a baking sheet and set aside. Cut the dough into 4 equal pieces. While working with the first piece, cover the remaining pieces with plastic wrap to keep them from drying out.

✳ Use your hand to shape the first piece of dough into a rectangle thin enough to feed into a pasta machine. Pass the dough through the machine on the widest setting. Repeat once more, then switch to the next thinnest setting and pass the dough through again, repeating for all of the settings until you get to the second thinnest (#7 on the Antree pasta maker attachment for the KitchenAid). Keep some flour on hand, as the dough can get sticky as you begin rolling it and you might need to reflour it as needed. Add the sheet of dough to the prepared baking sheet and repeat with the remaining dough.

✳ Heat a few inches of oil to 375°F in a large heavy pot over medium heat.

✳ Meanwhile, shape the cookies. Use a fluted pastry cutter to cut each sheet of dough widthwise into 2-inch-wide strips. Make a 1-inch slit down the center of each strip, then very carefully bring one end of the dough under and through the slit so it looks like a little twist. Since these cook quickly, you will want to have a good number of them, if not all of them, shaped before you start to fry.

✳ When the oil is ready, carefully drop 4 or 5 chiacchiere into the oil. Cook until puffed and deeply golden brown on each side, about 40 seconds total. Use a kitchen spider or slotted spoon to transfer the cooked chiacchiere to a paper-towel-lined baking sheet and heavily dust them with powdered sugar. Repeat with the remaining chiacchiere.

NOTE

You could roll these out by hand instead of using a pasta machine. You want the dough to be almost see-through but not too thin or else it will tear and won't puff.

Olive Oil
APPLE
Snack Cake

I call this a snack cake because there's no icing or topping, just a gratifyingly dense but not heavy cake that's impeccably moist and just the right amount of sweet thanks to the combination of apples and olive oil. Plus, it is just as appropriate for grazing on between meals as it is served after a meal. But what I love best about this recipe is how forgiving and foolproof it is. Nonna, who has never measured anything to save her life, makes this cake all the time, and will often switch up the ingredients: If she doesn't use milk, she'll use yogurt. If she doesn't feel like using yogurt, she'll use ricotta. No matter what, it comes out beautifully. You just slice, put it in a napkin, and carry on with your day.

❋ Preheat the oven to 350°F. Lightly coat an 8-inch springform pan with cooking spray and line the bottom with a round of parchment paper.

❋ In a large bowl with a hand mixer (or in a stand mixer fitted with the whisk), combine the sugar, oil, and eggs and whisk on medium speed until the ingredients are completely emulsified, about 2 minutes. Add the apples, milk, limoncello, vanilla, and lemon zest and mix until combined.

❋ Switch to a spatula or wooden spoon, add the flour, baking powder, and salt and stir until the dry ingredients are well incorporated. Pour the batter into the prepared pan and sprinkle about 1 tablespoon of sugar over the top.

❋ Bake until a toothpick inserted in the center comes out clean, about 45 minutes. Allow the cake to cool in the pan for about 30 minutes.

❋ Carefully remove the sides of the pan and transfer the cake (still on the cake bottom) to a wire rack to cool completely before serving. I keep this cake tightly covered at room temperature for up to 3 days, but it's really best eaten within a day or two of baking.

Cooking spray

1 cup sugar, plus more for sprinkling

¾ cup extra-virgin or light olive oil (I prefer extra-virgin)

2 large eggs

2 medium Honeycrisp apples, peeled and grated on the large holes of a box grater

¼ cup whole milk

2 tablespoons limoncello (optional; see Note), homemade (page 265) or store-bought

1 tablespoon pure vanilla paste or extract

Grated zest of 1 lemon

2 cups all-purpose flour

2 teaspoons baking powder

½ teaspoon kosher salt

NOTE
If you omit the limoncello, add 2 additional tablespoons milk.

SORBETTO
al Limone

7 lemons, washed and scrubbed well

1¼ cups sugar

Shot of limoncello (optional), homemade (page 265) or store-bought

Picture sitting by the Mediterranean enjoying a scoop of ice-cold, brightly lemon-flavored sorbet that's just the right balance of sweet and tart—that's exactly what this is (minus the body of water). It's the dreamiest warm-weather treat, especially when served in hollowed-out frozen lemons, which is what we do in Italy. And what makes this already simple recipe even simpler is that you can use an easy ratio to make any amount of it: Start with however many lemons you have, juice them, then add an equal volume of sugar and water. Done. Just don't skip blending the sorbet, which is the secret to achieving a texture that's light and airy instead of dense and icy.

✳ Grate the zest from 1 of the lemons and set aside (save the zested lemon for another use).

✳ Slice a very thin sliver from the bottom of each of the remaining 6 lemons so it sits firmly and doesn't wobble. Be careful not to cut off so much peel that it exposes the fruit. Then slice just enough from the top of each lemon so you can see the fruit.

✳ Use a small paring knife to carefully cut around the edges of the lemon where the flesh meets the white pith to loosen it, then use a spoon to gently scoop the fruit out from the peel, being careful not to tear the skin. Add the lemon pulp to a small bowl.

✳ Line a baking sheet with parchment paper. Arrange the hollowed-out lemon shells on the prepared baking sheet and pop them into the freezer.

✳ Squeeze the pulp through a lemon squeezer to extract the juice. Measure out 1¼ cups of the juice and save any remaining for another use.

✳ In a small saucepan, combine the sugar and 1¼ cups water. Cook over medium-low heat until the sugar dissolves (but don't bring to a boil), about 2 minutes. Remove the pan from the heat, stir in the reserved lemon zest, and set aside to cool completely.

✳ Once cooled, in a medium bowl, combine the simple syrup with the lemon juice. Cover and refrigerate overnight or up to 24 hours. If your ice cream machine requires you to freeze the insert, do that now.

✳ Add the lemon mixture and limoncello (if using) to a blender and blend on high for 1 minute. Pour the mixture into your ice cream machine and freeze according to the manufacturer's instructions.

✳ Scoop the frozen sorbet into the frozen lemons and return them to the freezer for about 1 hour to firm up. Serve icy cold.

NOTE

To make smaller servings, you can slice the lemons in half lengthwise, scoop out both halves, freeze the hollowed-out lemons, then top each half with a scoop of sorbet.

Boozy *Strawberries*

1 pound sweet ripe
strawberries, sliced
(I like the slices on the
thicker side)

2 tablespoons Nonna's
Limoncello (recipe
follows) or store-bought
limoncello (see Notes)

2 tablespoons sugar

Juice of ½ lemon

Nonna has always made her own limoncello, or lemon-infused vodka, so there was never a time when it wasn't around and never a time when a shot of that limoncello wouldn't find its way into anything and everything. In the spring and summer, it was all about letting it soak into fresh fruit—peaches, melon, blackberries—but at the center of it all were strawberries. She'd serve them topped with whipped cream or sorbet, on top of Migliaccio Napoletano (page 239) or Zeppole e Panzerotti (page 47), or on their own. Even from a young age I've loved these (yes, I know, I know), but they really are the perfect mix of a little sweet, a little sour, and a little, well, boozy.

NOTES

It can be hard to find a store-bought version, but I strongly encourage you to make your own!

Nonna would often make these berries with mandarinello, which is limoncello made with mandarin oranges (my personal favorite).

If serving these berries to children, or anyone who would prefer to not have alcohol, substitute the juice of 1 orange for the limoncello.

✳ In a medium bowl, toss the strawberries with the limoncello, sugar, and lemon juice. Cover with plastic wrap and refrigerate for at least 10 minutes before serving. Or you could make them in the morning and serve them in the evening; they get better the longer they sit.

Nonna's Limoncello

10 large wax-free
organic lemons, washed
and dried (see Notes)

4 cups 100-proof vodka
(I like Svedka or Absolut)

3½ cups sugar

NOTES

*You could also experiment
with different flavors by
using clementines, oranges,
or a mix of citrus fruits
instead of lemon.*

*If you like to think ahead—
as I do—this makes great
Christmas presents. When
I give them as gifts, I like
the tall bottles with a
swing-top stopper, either
17 ounces or 8 ounces.*

Not a year goes by when Nonna doesn't put up all her different "cellos," or limoncello and all the variations she makes with different fruit. After 6 weeks of soaking, it becomes a slightly sweet fruit-infused liquor that you can enjoy over ice at the end of a meal, drizzle over fresh fruit, or—Nonna's secret weapon—dilute with a little water and brush over a freshly baked cake to keep it moist and give it mild fruit flavor. My uncle Tony was kind enough to extract this recipe from her, which I now use faithfully every single year.

✳ Carefully peel the zest (colored layer) off the lemons in strips with a vegetable peeler, taking are to not get any of the spongy white pith underneath—this will make your limoncello bitter. Reserve the lemons for another use. (I like to freeze the juice in 1 tablespoon cubes and add it wherever I need fresh lemon juice. Same goes for limes—instant margaritas!)

✳ In a 6- to 8-cup bottle or jar with a tight-fitting lid, combine the vodka and lemon zest strips. Cover, shake, and store in a cool dark place (I put mine in the bottom of my pantry) for 3 weeks. Give it a shake daily.

✳ When ready to bottle, make the simple syrup. In a large pot, combine the sugar and 4 cups water. Cook over low heat until the sugar dissolves but doesn't boil, about 10 minutes. Remove the pot from the heat and allow the syrup to cool completely to room temperature.

✳ Strain the vodka, discard the lemon zest strips, and combine the vodka with the cooled simple syrup. Bottle the limoncello (see Notes) and refrigerate for 2 months before serving. Continue to store in the refrigerator, or stash yours in the freezer like I do.

CHESTNUTS
Two Ways

At the beginning of every November, my grandfather's best friend, Vittorio—the farmer he would barter with for fresh vegetables— would bring us crates of chestnuts from his trees. We'd roast them in the fireplace, usually with me sitting on Nonno's lap, and have them along with a bowl of clementines. Or we'd have them my mother's favorite way, which was boiled with bay leaves until they were easy to peel and buttery soft. When my husband, Joe, and I moved into our home in New Jersey and discovered that our neighbor had chest- nut trees, it felt like it was a sign from above that I was in exactly the right place. Now our neighbor brings me a couple bags full when the weather starts to get chilly, and for a blissful moment, I'm back in front of the fire with Nonna and Nonno.

✳ *Prepare the roasted chestnuts:* Preheat the oven to 375°F.

✳ Fill a large saucepan halfway with water and bring to a boil over medium-high heat.

✳ Use a chestnut scorer or a small sharp paring knife to score the rounded side of the chestnuts with an X. Set aside.

✳ Once the water comes to a boil, add the chestnuts and cook for 1 minute. Drain and transfer the chestnuts to a baking sheet. Slice, place into the oven, and roast until tender, 40 to 45 minutes. Take one out and test it by seeing if the peel comes off easily. When ready, immediately wrap the chestnuts tightly in a kitchen towel and let them sit for 10 minutes, which will make them easier to peel. Peel while still warm and enjoy.

✳ *Prepare the boiled chestnuts:* Using a small sharp paring knife, peel the thick outer shells of the chestnuts.

✳ In a large saucepan, combine the chestnuts with water to cover by a few inches. Add the bay leaves and salt and bring to a boil. Reduce the heat to medium-low and simmer until the chestnuts are tender, about 30 minutes.

✳ Drain the chestnuts and remove the thin inner skin, which should come right off. Enjoy warm.

Roasted Chestnuts
1½ pounds firm chestnuts

Boiled Chestnuts
1½ pounds firm chestnuts

2 bay leaves

Pinch of kosher salt

ACKNOWLEDGMENTS

To Raquel Pelzel and my wonderful team at Clarkson Potter, thank you for believing in me and helping me turn this dream of a book into a reality. I'm forever grateful you trusted me, and it's been a dream once again to work with you all!

To Rachel Holtzman, I simply couldn't have done this without you. You were my copilot and confidante throughout this process, and I will never accurately be able to describe how thankful I am for your help, your brilliant insight, and ability to put my words, heart, and soul on paper. Your brilliant mind and kind heart made this book possible, and I am forever in your debt!

This book wouldn't be the gorgeous masterpiece it is without the wildly talented Lauren Volo behind the lens. Your expertise, passion, and efforts to always go above and beyond in every shot have not gone unnoticed. I love calling you the "goddess of light," and these photos are proof as to why. Nobody does it better than you! Thank you, also, to Christina Zhang for helping everything come together so smoothly at the shoot.

To the incredible women who this book wouldn't be what it is without: the brilliant Maeve Sheridan, for understanding so clearly the vision for this book and making all my dreams come true with your talent to style each dish oh-so-perfectly and never missing an opportunity to fluff a napkin just right. You are pure magic, my friend! To Mira Evnine (and Megan Litt and Lauren Utvich), there are no words to describe my gratitude to you. Without you, your passion, attention to detail, and excitement for each dish, this book wouldn't be as beautiful as it is. It is because of you all that this book is a dream come true in every way. I will be forever grateful.

To my agent, Sabrina Taitz, and my WME team, thank you for pushing me to create the book of my dreams and guiding me along the way. I would have been lost without you!

To my followers and fellow Italian food lovers, this book is a love letter to my childhood and the people in my life who mean the most. I hope when you read it you will fall in love with all things Italian and get to know me on a deeper level. Thank you for your years and years of support, encouragement, love, and joy; none of these wild dreams would be possible without you; I will always be so thankful for your unwavering support!

To my friends and family, thank you for helping me bring a piece of Italy to life. It is my purpose in life to make you all feel loved, supported, and appreciated, and that my home be your comfort zone and my table be your safe place. Thank you for spending your weekends, birthdays, and holidays at my table; I will cherish our memories forever and can't wait to make new ones!

To my parents, thank you for always reminding me to be true to who I am. I wouldn't be able to accomplish my dreams if you didn't instill in me the importance of being unapologetically me.

To my nonna, this book is a love letter to you. Thank you for teaching me the importance of life, both in and out of the kitchen, for loving me unconditionally, and for always being there for me no matter how far apart we are geographically. These recipes have shaped us all, and my hope is that your legacy will now live in everyone else's home, too. Ti voglio un mondo di bene, nonnina mia!

To Joe and Mia, you two will always and forever be my biggest dream come true. Joe, I love that you take my love for "Italy in New Jersey" so seriously, stopping at nothing to make my dreams come true. This all started from you believing in me before I ever did. To my precious girl, it is my hope and dream that one day, when you have a home of your own, you'll turn to this book and read through it with a smile on your face, remembering all the days I've made you your favorite things and all the memories that came with it. My life is forever dedicated to loving you both.

INDEX